MUSICAL INSTRUMENT MAKERS OF AMERICA

Published by
Könemann Verlagsgesellschaft mbH
Bonner Straße 126 - D - 50968 Köln

Heart & Hands: Musical Instrument Makers of America

© 1999 by Könemann Verlagsgesellschaft mbH
© Photographs by Jake Jacobson
Northlight of Colorado, Inc.
P.O. Box 3809
Telluride, Colorado 81435, U.S.A.

Phone 970.728.6660

www.northlightofco.com

Design and Production by Media 27, Inc., Santa Barbara, California, U.S.A.
Printing and binding : Jean Lamour, Maxéville

Printed in France

ISBN 3-8290-2408-8

10 9 8 7 6 5 4 3 2 1

HEART & HANDS

MUSICAL INSTRUMENT MAKERS OF AMERICA

PHOTOGRAPHY BY JAKE JACOBSON

FOREWORD BY BILLY TAYLOR

RESEARCH & COLLABORATION BY TRISJA MALISOFF

EDITED BY NANCY ELLIS & ROBERT BAILEY

PRODUCED BY NORTHLIGHT OF COLORADO, INC.

PUBLISHED BY KÖNEMANN VERLAGSGESELLSCHAFT MBH

FOREWORD / BILLY TAYLOR

When I first heard about *Heart & Hands: Musical Instrument Makers of America*, I was very interested in the project because it featured so many individuals who are inventing new ways of doing things, who are pursuing something quite different from the ordinary.

Jake Jacobson's *Heart & Hands* tells the kind of story that would have had great appeal to my dear friend Charles Kuralt, who constantly sought out the interesting among ordinary people.

I have always believed that art chooses certain people, rather than the other way around; art is something you are compelled to do, and while the path you take may seem to defy logic to the rest of the world, it is entirely natural to the artist. Featured in the following pages are men and women of all ages, and from all walks of life, who make musical instruments for their own personal reasons. This is the basis of what I do as a jazz musician; the very act of creating jazz is highly personal, and it is as different for each musician as his or her own handwriting.

Today in the fast pace impersonal atmosphere of high technology we need to look more often at the creative and unique things being done by ordinary people. In *Heart & Hands*, it is a pleasure to meet these makers who are not just low-key, but who have chosen to devote their lives to something they love—not to get rich or to astound, but because they simply love what they do.

There is another benefit to the kind of celebration contained in *Heart & Hands*. Through Jacobson's photographs and their own words, these musical instrument makers provide inspiration; they set an example for others who may be considering the possibility of following their own hearts.

Billy Taylor, prominent jazz musician, arts educator and long-time correspondent for CBS Sunday Morning, lives in New York City. Winner of numerous fellowships and awards, he played with most of the great jazz musicians during the 1940s and '50s, earned a doctorate from the University of Massachusetts, and continues a distinguished career as both a performer and educator. He is Artistic Advisor for Jazz to the John F. Kennedy Center for the Performing Arts in Washington, D.C., and founder of Jazz Models and Mentors, now into its second decade at the Metropolitan Museum of Art in New York.

GLEN JOHNSTON
Studio City, California

PREFACE / JAKE JACOBSON

The inspiration for this project actually began when I was 12 years old, and first walked into the Studio City studio of my saxophone teacher, Glen Johnston. It was impossible for me to imagine at that moment the important role this gentleman would come to play in my life. Glen became more than a teacher; he was a true mentor, introducing me to the richness, passion and variety of the language of music. He also taught me a lot about life. Glen was a man of great dignity who had a wonderful sense of humor. Friends and fellow musicians enjoyed visiting his studio, and even as a teenager, I was often invited to listen to sessions of the world-class musicians who would gather there, where he also repaired and rebuilt instruments and mouthpieces. Many years later, I honored Glen Johnston in a short black and white film titled *The Mouthpiece Man.*

My fascination for behind the scenes instrument making has never left me, and in 1996, more than 20 years later, encouraged by *National Geographic* photographer Sam Abell during a workshop in Santa Fe, I decided to undertake the project that has become *Heart & Hands: Musical Instrument Makers of America.*

Words cannot describe what it was like to visit with more than 250 craftspeople throughout America, to see and touch the beautiful and often innovative instruments these men and women have devoted their lives to making, and to hear their histories, their hopes and their dreams. Accompanied by researcher and collaborator Trisja Malisoff, we were welcomed into their homes and workshops, we were fed and feted, and witness to an astonishing variety of information about music, art and America. We were also treated to some of the most incredible and intimate musical performances of our lives. The hardest part—each and every time—was leaving our new friends.

Themes quickly began to emerge, and not surprisingly, money was a common one: Virtually no one gets into instrument making "for the money." Not that they aren't able to make a living this way, because many of these makers do, but they all seem to agree that "it's a poor way to try to get rich." Nevertheless, I met some of the happiest people I've ever encountered, people who do what they do simply because they love it, because it's important for them to "give back" in life, to give pleasure and joy to others. I met one old maker who won't accept money; he gives his fiddles away to a selected few whom he knows will appreciate and use his gift. In a California prison program, I met convicted murderers who have found redemption through learning to make guitars. I met artisans who recycle junk into musical instruments, and many who are passionate and dedicated to teaching children that music is for everyone, not just a privileged few. I met makers whose instruments are used as powerful tools for healing.

The political power of music, and historic repression of it—especially among Native Americans, who were stripped of their traditions and forbidden for so many years to make or play their instruments—is another recurrent theme among musical instrument makers. The banjo, traditionally an African gourd instrument, came to America through the horror of slavery. In Jamaica, where the British forbade natives to play instruments, an entirely new form of music was born as recently as the 1950s—steel drums—adapted from trash, discarded military oil barrels readily available even to the poorest among them. Technologies such as sonar, x-ray and MRI provide modern-day makers with unprecedented access to information. The internet has opened up vast new marketing possibilities. Indeed, some makers virtually do all their sales over the internet, as well as locating parts and communicating with fellow makers.

The desire to experiment is another strong theme among instrument makers, who have the courage to innovate, to make things differently, and to make different things. Included here are a number of experimental makers and *avant garde* artists who create sound sculpture, and others who dare design new shapes for traditional instruments. We found an amazing variety of ethnicity and universal appreciation for the freedoms that are at the foundation of this country. The cross-section of instruments made in the United States—European, African, Eastern, Oriental, Aboriginal, Latin—reaffirms that America is indeed a true melting pot, and music *is* the universal language.

The level of intimacy we encountered as instrument makers bared their souls to us was intense, and at times we found ourselves shedding tears along with some of them, mourning a lost child, a dearly beloved spouse or a faithful pet. In Tennessee, a mandolin maker who had not set foot in his studio since his wife died, wrote later that our visit had sparked his decision to return to work. Some of the best gospel music I ever heard in my life was played on the mandolin for us by a maker in Berea, Kentucky. Included here also are dedicated employees from some of America's musical instrument factories, such as Steinway Pianos and Martin Guitars. In Elkhart, Indiana many factories still produce some of the finest woodwinds and brass instruments in the world.

There was enormous gratitude among instrument makers for the unusual focus of *Heart & Hands*—on craftspeople you almost never hear about, and certainly never see. One bagpipe maker commented that the names on our list included many people he knew professionally, "but only through phone conversations; I've never actually met them, so your book will be a pictorial introduction!"

Heart & Hands is not intended to be *the* definitive list of musical instrument makers in America; there are hundreds, probably thousands of other makers who were not interviewed during our more than two-year cross-country trek. *Heart & Hands* is about people who have chosen to dedicate their lives to something they love, often at great personal sacrifice. Virtually no one we met is looking for ways to cut corners in their instrument making; there is tremendous dedication to ensure the highest quality craft and sound, and the makers seem to always be looking for ways to improve on both.

This joyous journey throughout America has re-affirmed to me the philosophy of my teacher Glen Johnston: *"When you play from the heart, you can't be out of tune."* Hopefully, through these photographs and excerpts of their interviews, you too, will share in honoring these dedicated individuals—these truly unsung heroes—who represent the very essence of American artistry and ingenuity.

JAKE JACOBSON
Telluride, Colorado, 1998

INTRODUCTION / TRISJA MALISOFF

The road to fine craftsmanship is narrow, a trail of divine inspiration to artful creation. It is a journey precious few navigate successfully. I never anticipated at the outset the full impact this project would have on me. We were welcomed into artisan homes with coffee, a meal, a song played on instruments by their creator. This book is an invitation to appreciate their craft, to understand their motivation, to glimpse their souls. It is said where there is music there can be no evil; certainly the experience of our travels confirmed this truth.

Fine craftsmanship knows no common political, religious, economic, or color consensus. As artistic and creative ability has no boundaries, only music is the common thread interwoven from one artisan to another. It is a song sung in many different keys, in different dialects, on different instruments. It is a shared passion for music with the art of the craft. They touched me in a profound way, I still follow many along their path of inspiration. These are the hands of the heart of America. Here we feel and hear the inspiration of our country. We see through their eyes the glory of our nation, the expression of our individual freedom. From the resonance of a fiddle, the whisper of a flute, or the strum of a guitar we hear the voices of our collective soul. It is American; it is free, it is proud, it is unique. We see through their eyes, feel through their hands, hear through their ears and know the place of their heart.

I am grateful to the artists, artisans, folklorists, and others for their contributions. Numerous public and private agencies took the time and effort to help locate each talented craftsperson documented here. Many more master technicians have fallen through the cracks without receiving the recognition they deserve. I regret we were unable to reach and photograph more artists. Recognition never was part of their repertoire or an influence of their creation. If anything, it is enough to know each has crafted instruments capable of reproducing the sound of an angel's flight. Perhaps this book can serve as inspiration to future artisans to continue our proud and noble cultural heritage. For heart and hands to be joined, ears must hear and eyes must see.

Trisja Malisoff
Pacific Palisades, California, 1998

I dedicate my journey for this book to my son Ben, who walked to his own drummer while I was working on this project.

I would like to personally acknowledge:

To Jake Jacobson, whose vision extended an opportunity to meet the most amazing people imaginable. The two and half years are a life long gift.

To Patty Theis who synchronized with Ben during my absences.

To John and Jill Walsh for their knowledge and contagious enthusiasm.

To Robert Bailey whose original ideas extend themselves to type.

My heartfelt thanks to all my friends and family for their support and patience with me during this project.

The staff at Smithsonian Institution Traveling Exhibition Service for recognizing the archival importance of this project. Their professionalism and vision were unyielding.

And finally, to all the instrument makers: who took the time to tell their stories, to open their hearts and to allow a glimpse of amazing talent and craftsmanship. They are the true heroes of our time.

THE GULF REGION

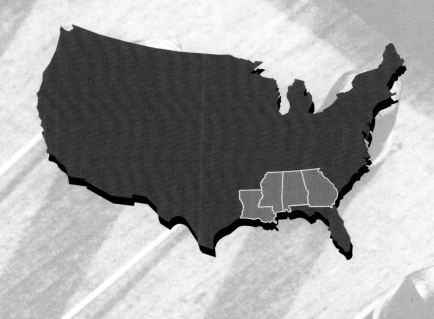

The Gulf region is a cultural kaleidoscope: African. European. Creole. Arcadian. A swampy energy emanates

from the muddy, amniotic waters of the Mississippi, the womb from which the blues were borne. The Delta itself

is an amiable, inviting territory of ethnic diversity and musical tradition. A microcosm of American life, the area

is so rich in its musical influences that its like the proverbial large and friendly bloodhound on a small wooden porch;

every time it wags its tail it knocks over a rocking chair.

Families gather together, generation upon generation, to share music, voices and love. Hand-crafted instruments

abound. The craftsmanship can be as simple as the Diddley bow—bailing wire and two nails pounded into the side

of a barn—or as complex as the exquisite Baroque instruments built in the Gulf and sold throughout the world.

Robert Johnson called the Delta the Crossroads, where a man and a handmade guitar could challenge evil itself.

For us the Gulf States region was a starting point, the birth of a journey of both imagery and spirituality.

"Everything comes off the land.
I use cow bones... groundhog hides..."

JERRY KING, BLAIRSVILLE, GA

13

JERRY KING, BLAIRSVILLE, GA

OTHA TURNER, SENATOBIA, MS

"There was always music."

BOB BENEDETTO, EAST STROUDSBERG, PA

"This is gonna make people happy.
This is gonna play music."

FRANK FINOCCHIO, EASTON, PA

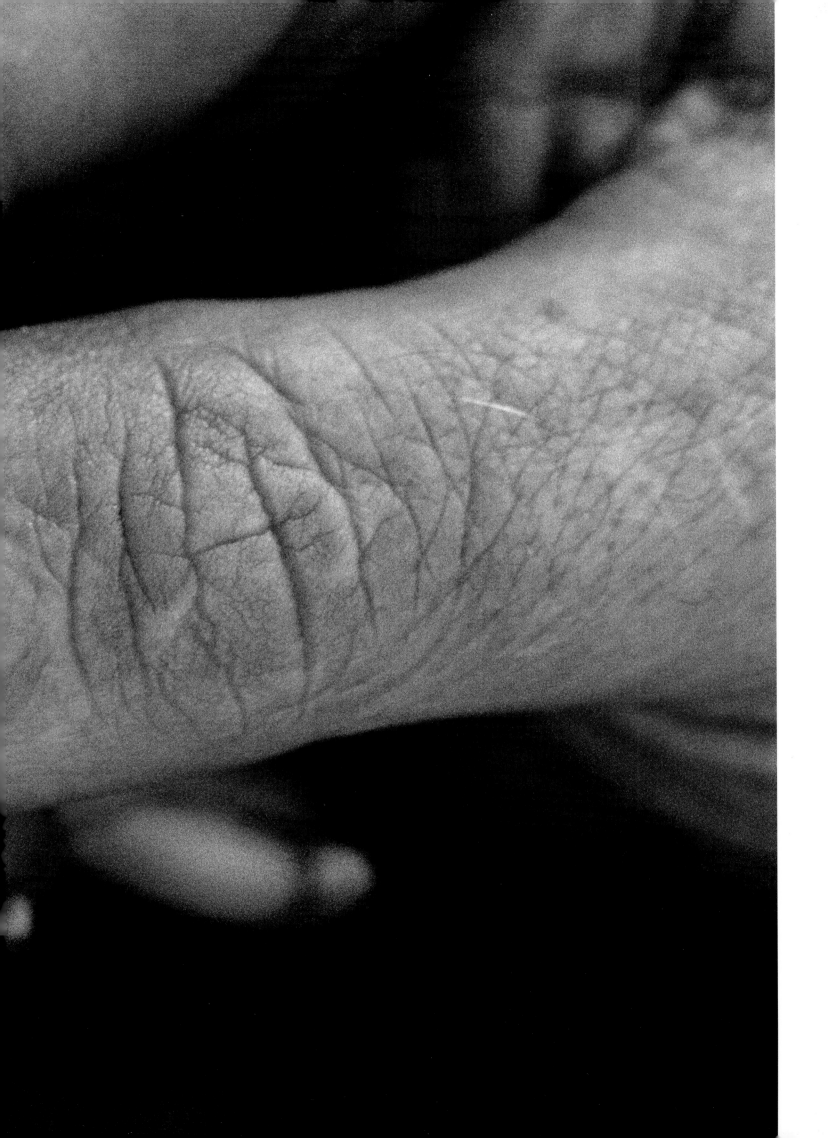

19

DICK RICHARD, CHURCH POINT, LA

"I tell ya, this rock-n-roll, them people that call it music, don't have any more talent than one of them chickens up yonder..."

ARLIN MOON, HOLLY POND, AL

"you and the guitar more or less becomes one as time goes on."

ROBERT NOONER, TRACY DEUEL VOCATIONAL INSTITUTION, TRACY, CA

TONY IANUARIO, JEFFERSON, GA

GENE IVEY, IDER, AL

29

"there's part of you in that instrument..."

HERB TAYLOR, CONYERS, GA

"I know who I am, where I've come from."

ROBERT MIRABAL, TAOS, NM

JERRY KING, BLAIRSVILLE, GA

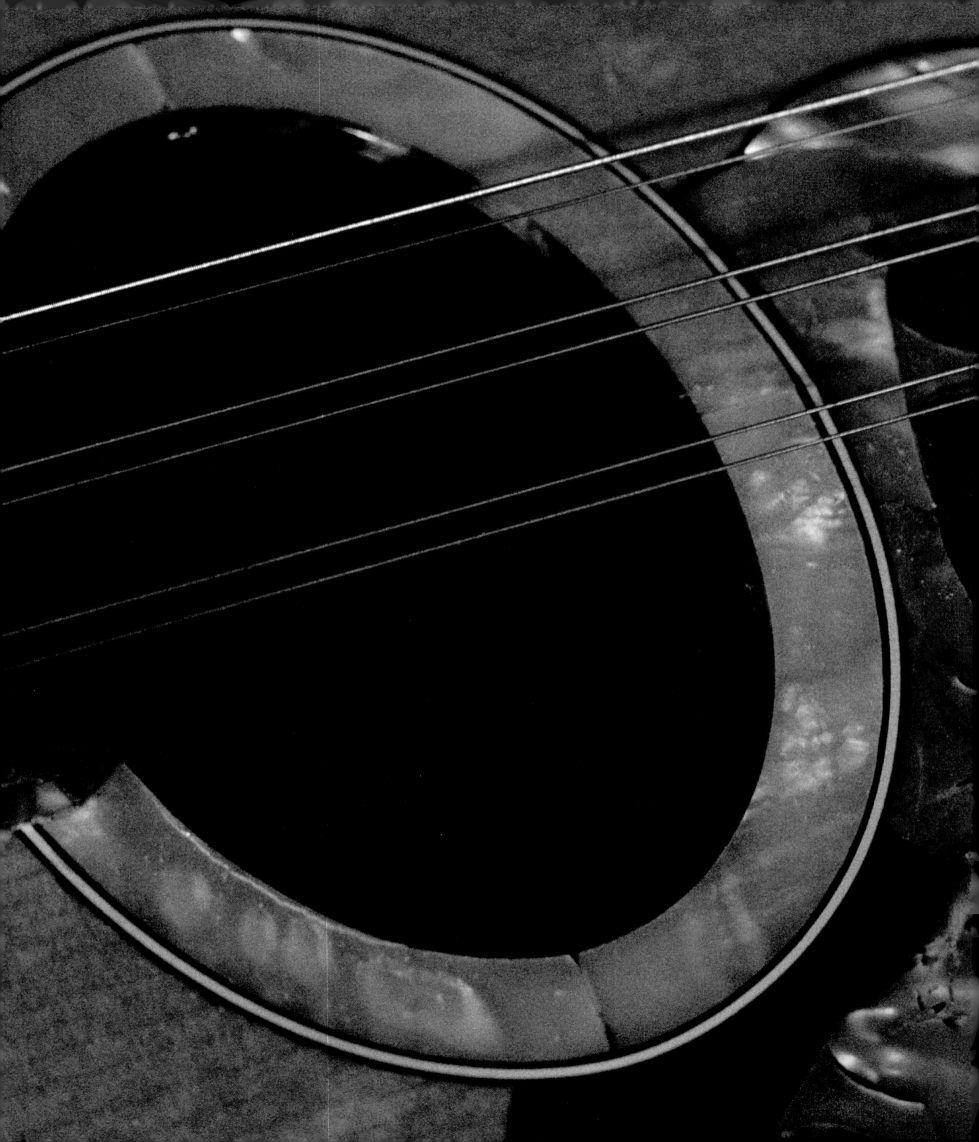

"...what the hell, I'll make my own."

BILL ALLEGRETTI, CLAYTON, DE

W. FURMAN THRONTON, HARTWELL, GA

JOHN HUTTO, AUGUSTA, GA

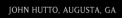

39

LUKE THOMPSON, ZACHARY, LA

"The fiddle is the king...

CHARLES JEAN HORNER, CUMBERLAND

DEBORAH-HELEN VIATOR,
JUAN MOÏSE VIATOR,
ALIDA MANUEL VIATOR,
EUNICE, LA

...ght, love..."

CONSTANDINO "DINO" BERSIS, NEW YORK CITY, NY

GREEN, LACEY SPRINGS, AL

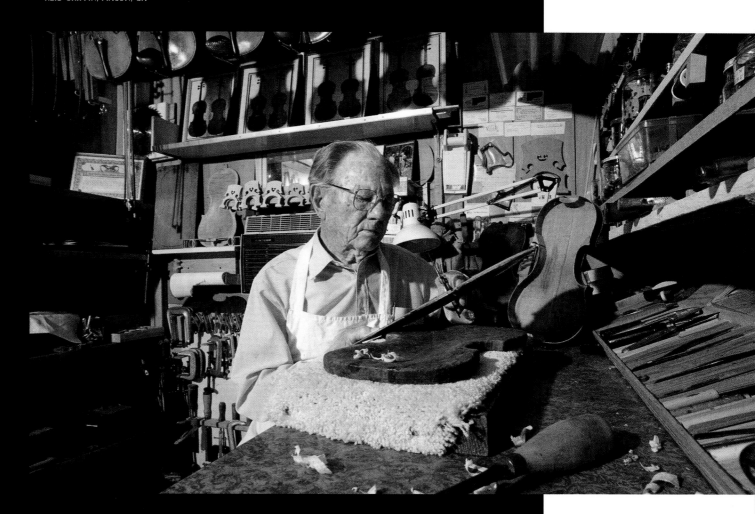

"I wouldn't trade my life for anything."

MURRAY HUGGINS, ASHLAND, OR

ADNER ORTEGO, WASHINGTON, LA

ear, I learn a little more."

DEWEY ALEXANDER, FOXWORTH, MS

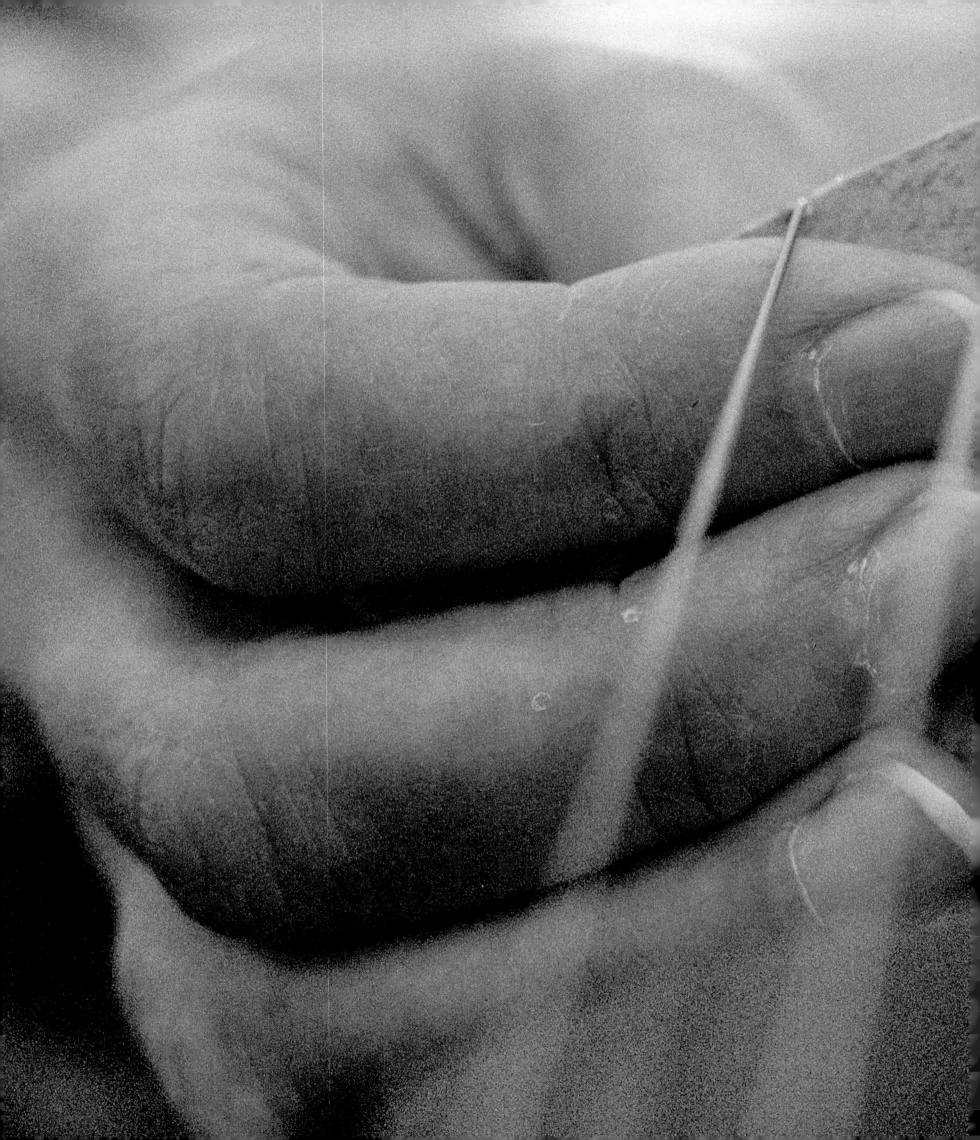

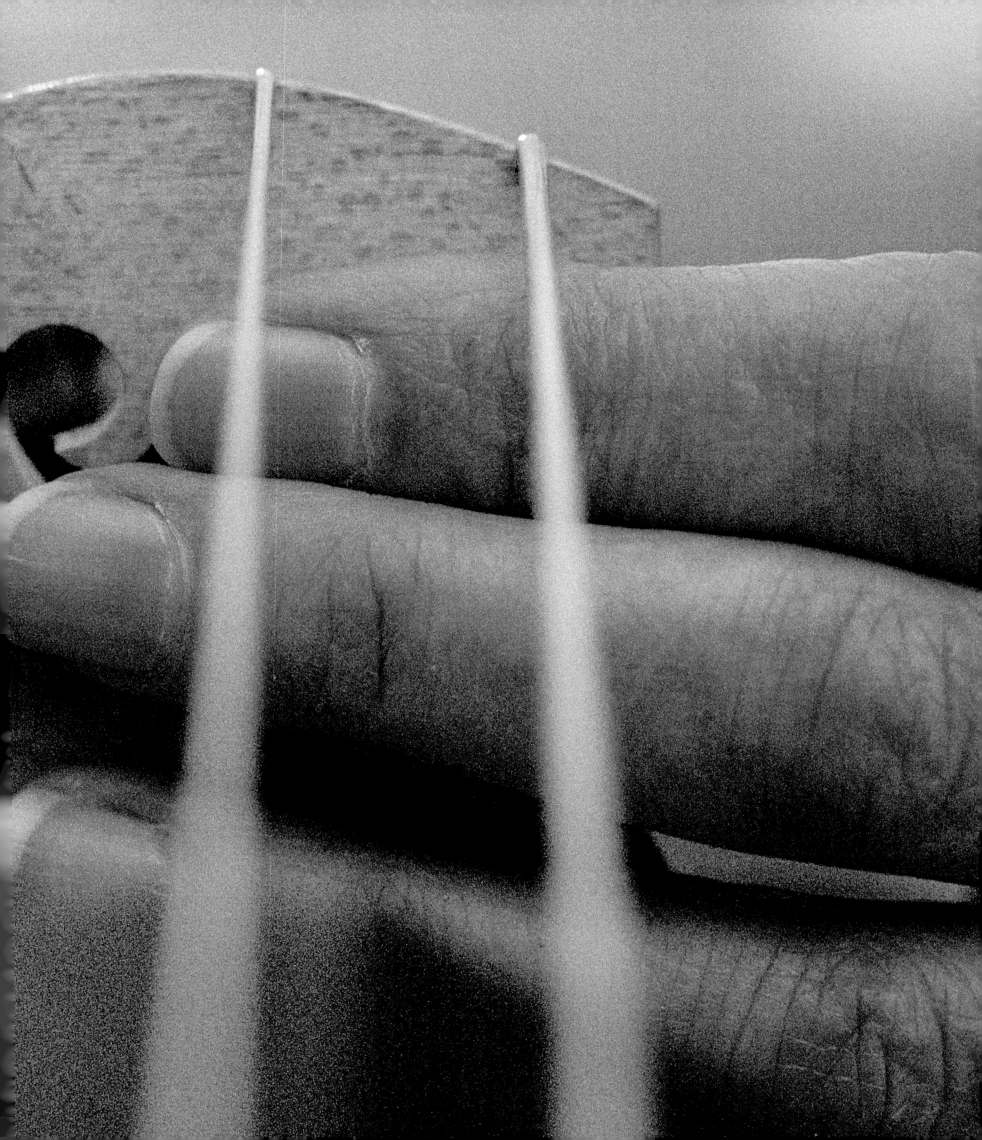

BARRY KRATZER AND MARK GRESHAM, SAVANNAH, GA

"...when you play it and it keeps ringing, that is good."

NATIVIDAD "NATE" TIRADO, NEW CASTLE, DE

ROYNE FONTENOT,
EUNICE, LA

HARRY A. VAS DIAS, DECATUR, GA

WALTER BISHOP, ATLANTA, GA

LARRY MILLER, IOTA, LA

"the sweetest sound you ever heard"

HERB TAYLOR, CONYERS, GA

61

JAMES "SUPERCHICKEN" JOHNSON, CLARKSDALE MS

RANDY WOOD, ISLE OF HOPE, GA

ER ORTEGO,
SHINGTON, LA

THE DELTA REGION

One of the things I really love to do is rescue old instruments. I've got one in there I was gonna show you if you're interested. I got it in a box in about 30 pieces. It's a very, very old violin. When I got it put together, it had the sweetest sound you ever heard...

HERB TAYLOR, CONYERS, GA

I don't buy anything except strings. Everything comes off the land. Some of the things I use is bones — cow bones. I use groundhog hides. Everything else comes right off the land here... A banjo's only a little drum with strings across, really.

JERRY KING, BLAIRSVILLE, GA

But if you build somethin'... If one of the instruments that I build, it may last a thousand years. Heck, it may last two or three thousand years. And somebody will look inside of it and say, "Well, there was a fellow, by the name of Joe Hosmer built this. Wonder where he's from..."

JOE HOSMER, HUEYTOWN, AL

I find I was born with art talent. It gnaws at me and it has to be relieved some way in some sort of artistic expression. So, I've built banjos since 1964 or 5...

BOB FLESHER, PEACHTREE CITY, GA

Yes Sir... It's a fishin' cane, that's what everybody call it, fishin' cane... That cane is green — you can take this cane when it's green and borrow a tune... Out of a green cane, gotta be a dry, seasoned cane to make a fife. You cannot make a fife out of one-jointed cane. This is one joint, see, see that joint there? You gotta get inside of this joint...

OTHA TURNER, SENATOBIA, MS

Working for yourself, you don't make any money, but you can at least *enjoy* not making any...

RANDY WOOD, ISLE OF HOPE, GA

...You stay focused on it, and if you stay focused on it for a number of years and through all these times when you love it and times when you hate it — and you gradually watch the work. You gradually get more recognition and if you hang onto it, it becomes very spiritual.

KENT EVERETT, CHAMBLEE, GA

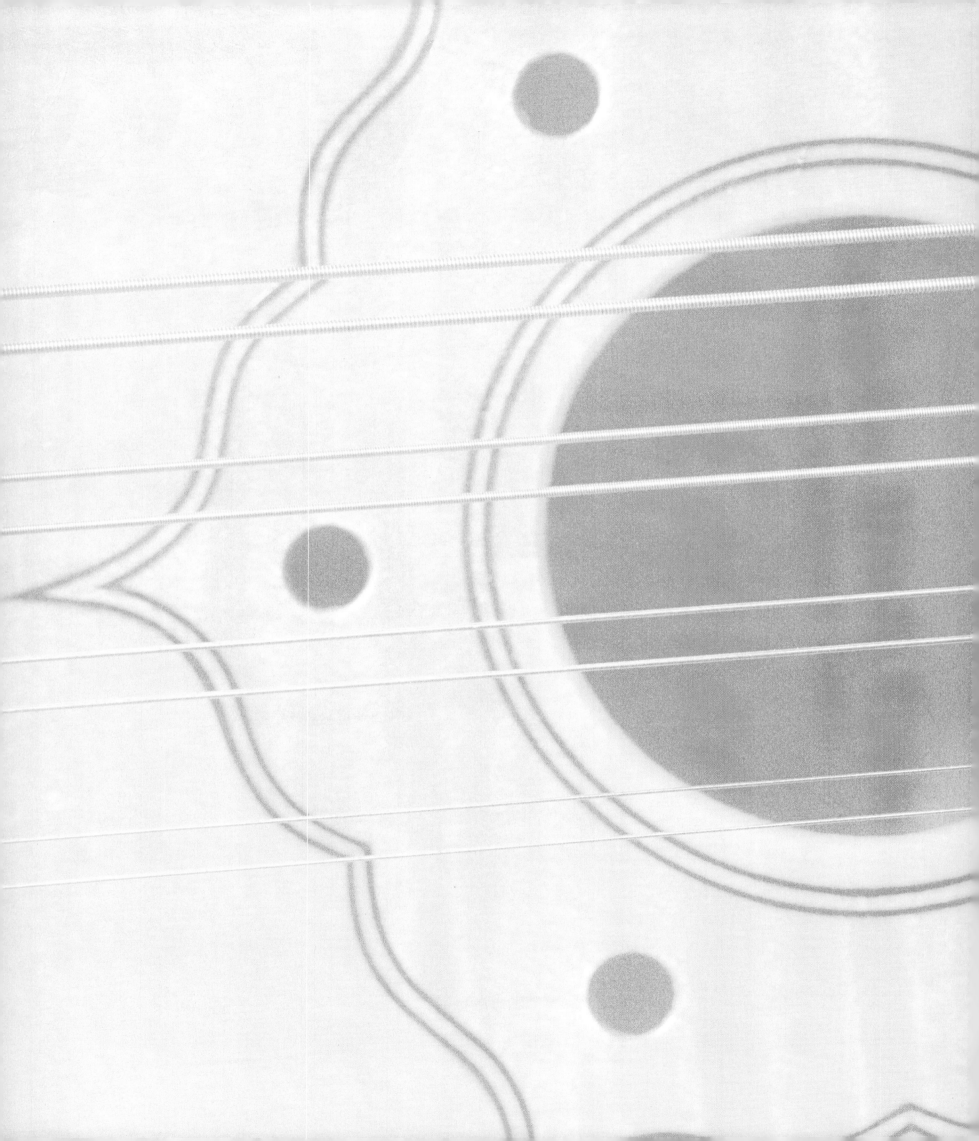

THE APPALACHIAN MOUNTAIN REGION

The Appalachian mountain people have a way of inventing tradition each morning and erasing the hardships of the past by nightfall, each circumstance accompanied by the resonant sound of a hand-crafted wooden instrument. No music is more uniquely American than mountain music. Smoke, smiles, and skill served up Southern family style; the sun, the sky, the stir of birds and insects—the entire region is an alliterative tone poem. The music has flourished since the earliest settlements and continues to play a major role in the daily lives of the people who live and work here.

The area today is replete with various traditional, folk, and bluegrass festivals and boasts more dedicated musical craftspeople than anywhere in the country. Many of these artisans live in isolated areas of astounding beauty where honesty and open-armed hospitality abound. While the rural areas of the region feature a focused seclusion that supports a rugged and lasting craftsmanship, Appalachia is also home to cosmopolitan centers that offer a sophisticated array of furniture and art.

Passionate and proud, mountain folk are dedicated to handing down their treasured traditions, revealing a musical and lyrical history as rich in theme as any handmade Appalachian quilt.

TOM FELLENBAUM, BLACK MOUNTAIN, NC

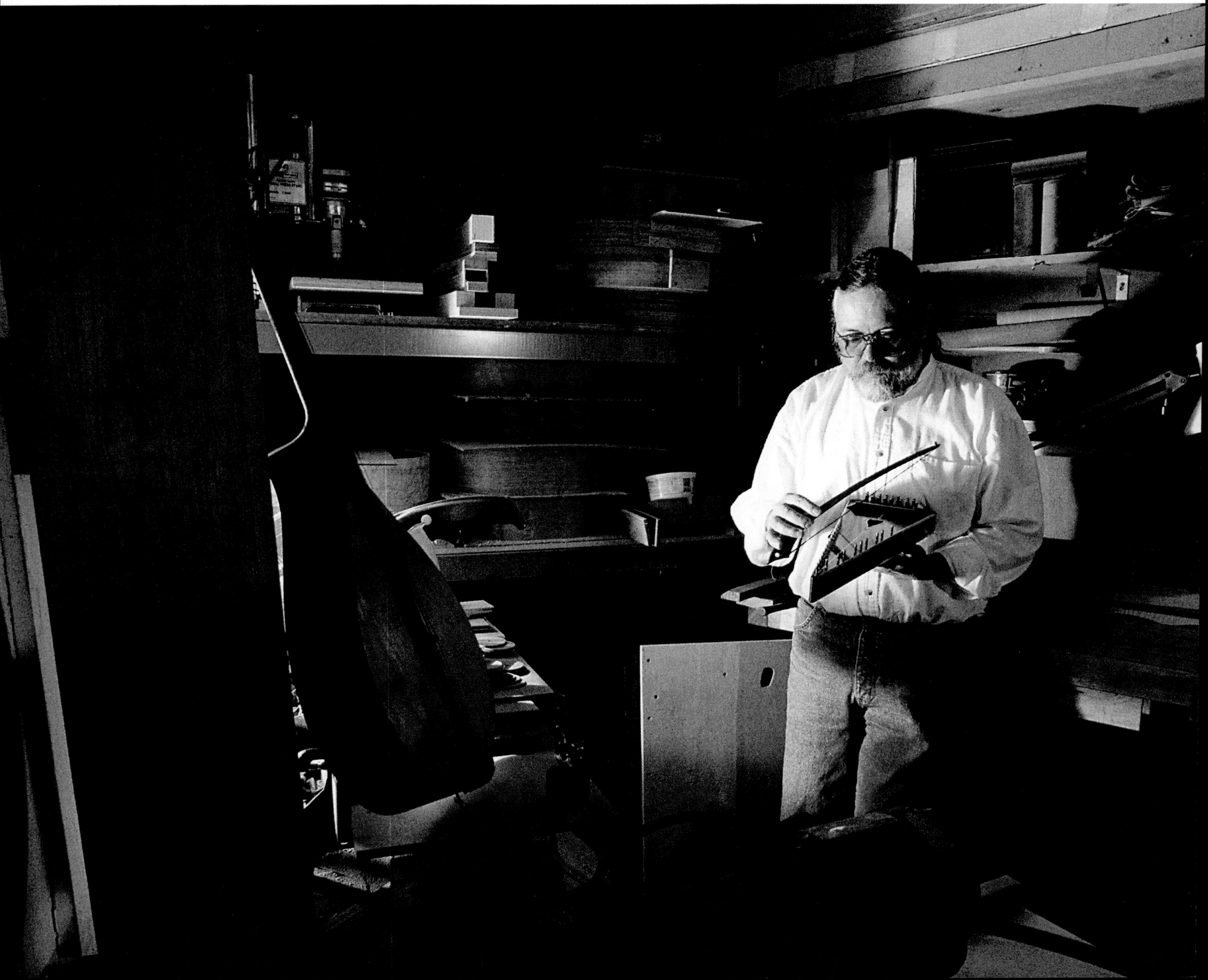

DON GALLAGHER, WARTRACE, TN

"...it's the best thing I do, and the most important thing I do, and the thing I want to do most..."

JOEL ECKHAUS, PORTLAND, ME

"Once you get into the guitar making field, there's a hook that doesn't let you go..."

TOM MORGAN,
DAYTON, TN

CHARLES JEAN HORNER, CUMBERLAND GAP, TN

"you got nothin' without a fiddle"

CHARLES JEAN HORNER, CUMBERLAND GAP, TN

FREEMAN JONES, OLD FORT, NC

"we stick to the old ways..."

J.W. HAM, ATHENS, AL

CLIFFORD GLENN, SUGAR GROVE, NC

"we pay attention to the
people who were here before us."

DELGADO FAMILY, EAST LOS ANGELES, CA

HOMER LEDFORD, WINCHESTER, KY

94

"...music in so many
different shades of color
and light that everybody
finds his own color to his
own liking and taste."

GEORGE KELISCHEK, BRASSTOWN, NC

"...you get down in them mountains they still got that bluegrass music... the real stuff."

JIMMY COX, TOPSHAM, ME

"...The more I make them, the more I
want to make them..."

JOSÉ FERNANDEZ, PROVIDENCE, RI

JANE FISTORI, BEREA, KY

BOB FISTORI, BEREA, KY

WILLIAM CRABTREE, STONE GAP, VA

o the best you can,

softly."

WARREN MAY, BEREA, KY

JAMES WILLIAMS, WOOTON, KY

"You take a piece
of wood, and you start
to tap it... oh, it rings...
Oh! This is the piece
I've been waiting for..."

FRANK FINOCCHIO, EASTON, PA

110

HAWK LITTLEJOHN, OLD FORT, NC

"...all music is folk music; it comes from the heart."

TOM FELLENBAUM, BLACK MOUNTAIN, NC

AUDREY HASH HAM, LANSING, NC

"Music is something that we're all capable of doing... everybody is creative. It's what being human is all about..."

JODY KRUSKAL, BROOKLYN, NY

WALTER MESSICK, WHITE TOP MOUNTAIN, VA

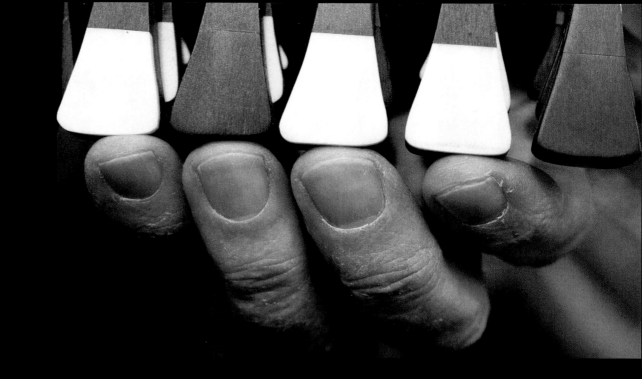

GLENN GREENE, KNOXVILLE, TN

THE APPALACHIAN MOUNTAIN REGION

When I grew up I followed Daddy around always...and I would sit and watch, but when I was in high school, girls did not take shop. I mean, that wasn't *done*. I wish I could have. I took home ec., and I can cook like a demon, but that didn't help with fiddle making... I worked on that dulcimer and I worked and I worked, and it was without a doubt, the ugliest instrument that anybody had ever seen! I mean, I didn't know how to do the neck; I didn't know—but it played. And it was hideous. I gave it to Daddy for his birthday. And he said, "Audrey, I would a lot rather had that than a brand new Cadillac." And I told him it was a darn good thing, because I couldn't ever buy him a Cadillac.

I made one for an old man—he knew the tone that he wanted and so forth, and tried to explain it to me, and I thought I had it, but I didn't know whether I understood what he was looking for in tone. OK, he came to get the fiddle and he sat down, my gosh, and he cried when he played it. And his wife was patting him on the back the whole time. And he treasured that. And that's the joy in it—it is to give something to someone that they can appreciate...

AUDREY HASH HAM, LANSING, NC

My musical project is called "make a joyful noise" and it's based on comin' up with simple, funky, home-made musical instruments with minimal learning curves...

ROBERT FRITO SEVEN, ASHEVILLE, NC

The older the instrument gets, the better it gets...

TOM MORGAN, DAYTON, TN

I make musical spoons and people pick them up at a show and, you know, tap'em two or three times on their leg and they'll go, "Well, I just don't have any rhythm." And I'll lean over real quiet and I'll say, "Your heart's beatin' i'n it?"

We are rhythm, everything's rhythm. Sun comes up, sun goes down, breathe in, breathe out. And so—my mission is to try to get people back in touch with that basic thing... Work with that tapping, then you build up a sense of timing. Playin' spoons is only playin' a hand drum...

ROBERT FRITO SEVEN, ASHEVILLE, NC

The old lute makers were living in a world where, you know, proportion and symmetry and geometry was really important to them, and they had, coming out of the humanistic tradition from the Renaissance, thought that their instruments had to be in tune with the universe, otherwise they wouldn't sound well... I don't have any damn *trade secrets*. But you find some who feel if they don't get full measure, full credit for being self made, it's somehow demeans what they might have accomplished.

This is a 5,000 years old tradition. How long has it been evolving, and how much have I benefited from what a thousand others have done?

JAMES TRANTHAM, CANTON, NC

People ask me why I want to build a cello. I guess the answer is because it is there. I have already made two and I can't sell them. Why do I bother? It's fun and I like to do it...

CAROLYN WILSON FIELD, OAK RIDGE, TN

Start out on a guitar first. And mama, she was playin' the dulcimer. She learned me chords and I'd play along with her, her playin' the dulcimer. Well, I wasn't satisfied with that. I said, "Mama, let me..." I'd stand behind her here. I'd beat them strings... And first thing I knowed, I was playin' a tune. Just a little feller...

JACOB RAY MELTON, GALAX, VA

I'm truly unemployable. I couldn't work for anybody. If I had skills anymore I couldn't work for 'em. I mean I can hardly work for myself! I don't want any bosses. I don't want to be told what to do and what not to do. Although I'll work seven days a week for myself. Life's too short...

WALTER MESSICK, WHITE TOP MOUNTAIN, VA

...there's not much to life unless, you know, you can not go all intent on how much money you can make, or whatever you want to do, but it doesn't mean a whole lot unless you can pick up something important and give back to share...

TOM MORGAN, DAYTON, TN

I like to compare music with a multi-faceted diamond ring reflecting the same thing. Music in so many different shades of color and light that everybody finds his own color for his own liking and taste.

GEORGE KELISCHEK, BRASSTOWN, NC

122

Here is the stuff on the instrument itself. It makes a beautiful sound. The more stuff you put on, the more sound you get out of it.

JAMES WILLIAMS, SLEMP, KY

The hammered dulcimer was brought back from the Middle East by the Crusaders to Western Europe. That dulcimer became the piano, the modern day piano. If you took the back off the piano, you would have a hammered dulcimer. And the Appalachian dulcimer is basically an American instrument and they had people who settled through the mountains who had their heritage in Scandinavia, England or Ireland. They all had a similar instrument. But the finished instrument as you see it is purely an American instrument.

The banjo had its, from what we understand, the slaves had gourd and skins that they stretched and had strings on, that they played. The banjo is the only other one you can say is really an American instrument—based on who changed it once they were here in this country.

WARREN MAY, BEREA, KY

The instrument is art, science, and math, but I look at it as *art*. I used to be a musician, but doing this all day makes me not feel like picking at night. I string them and make sure the frets don't buzz by playing a few chords and that's about it... I like making madolins, which I did for 12 years. I like making all kinds of instruments and it's fun. I'm diversified because a lot of people are not stuck on one type of guitar.

JIM TRIGGS

CONNECTICUT   DELAWARE   MAINE   MARYLAND
MASSACHUSETTS   NEW HAMPSHIRE   NEW JERSEY
NEW YORK   PENNSYLVANIA   RHODE ISLAND   VERMONT

THE NORTHEAST REGION

The Northeast is historically defined by its coastline, where the Pilgrims first answered the challenge of the New World. Nowhere else in America are the seasons so vividly defined; nowhere else can lay legitimate claim to the Yankee culture. To this region much has been given and much is required. The Northeast is the cradle of a country deliberately founded on a good idea. From the finest violin and cello makers to the oldest American manufacturers of flutes and pianos, the area offers an urbane and international musical perspective.

Here the musical melting pot includes Asian, African, and Jamaican craftspeople, alongside the strong traditions and influences of the English, Irish and Scottish. Many of the world's finest classical instrument makers work here, and even in a factory setting the individual devotion to fine craftsmanship is uncompromising.

From the national icons of its major cities to the dark rural beauty of its most isolated climes, the musical artisans of the Northeast reflect the region's independent attitudes and innovative self sufficiency.

"It's the human touch; that's what this is all about."

PETER WHITEHEAD, SAN FRANCISCO, CA

BOB BENEDETTO,
EAST STROUDSBERG, PA

JUAN "PEPE" SANTANA, STANHOPE, NJ

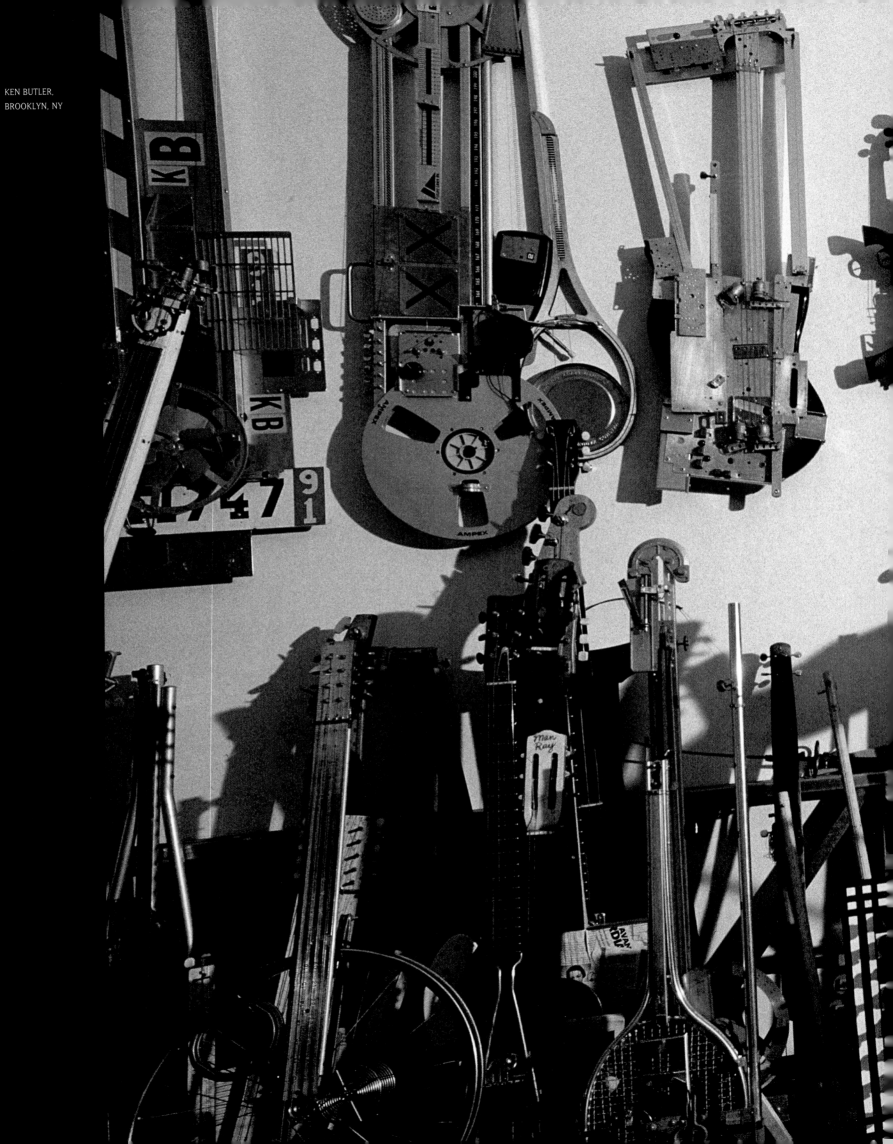

KEN BUTLER,
BROOKLYN, NY

"...every sound's a winner."

DWIGHT GRAVES, WARNER, NH

CHRISTIAN MARTIN IV, NAZARETH, PA

DICK BOAK, NAZARETH, PA

"...to me, the inside is really the most beautiful part of it."

ROBERT L. VINCENT, TRACY DEUEL VOCATIONAL INSTITUTION, TRACY, CA

EMPLOYEES AT MARTIN GUITARS, NAZARETH, PA

137

KARL M. DENNIS, WARREN, RI

"Everything about music
and about making instruments
should be for joy;
it should be for pleasure..."

PEANG KUONG, PHILADELPHIA, PA

BILL LOVELESS, BELTSVILLE, MD

145

ROBERT SHADE AND BILL LOVELESS, BELTSVILLE, MD

DEENA ZALKIND SPEAR, ACCOKEEK, MD

"you get this inner peace from inside..."

DEENA ZALKIND SPEAR & ROBERT SPEAR, ACCOKEEK, MD

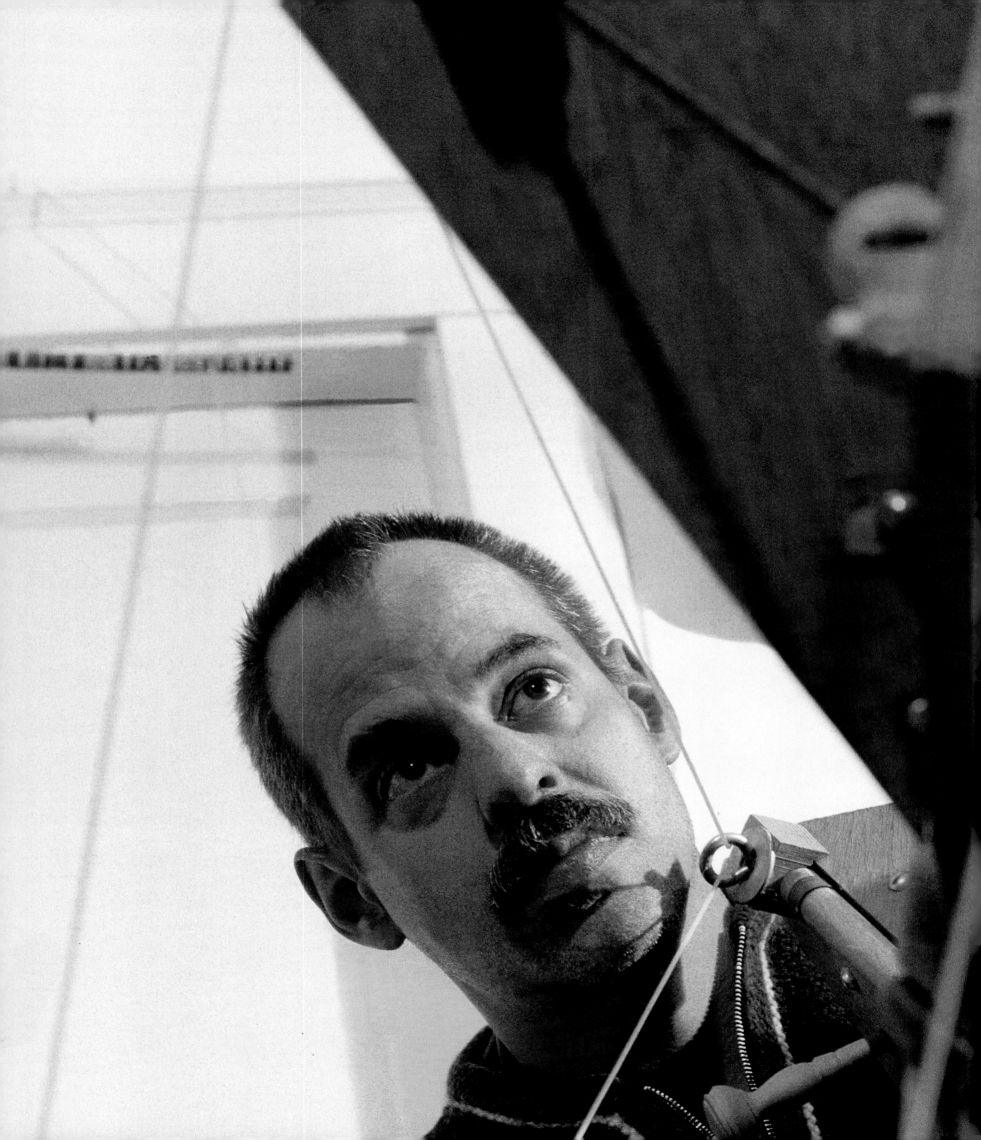

DMYTRO SOROCHANIUK & HALYNA STEFURAK-KARAMAN, PENNSAUKEN, NJ

"When you really want something,
you just go for it."

JOSÉ FERNANDEZ, PROVIDENCE, RI

MICHAEL DOW, YORK, ME

EMPLOYEE AT ZILDJIAN CYMBALS, NORWELL, MA

"Steinways will last hundreds of years;
they just cannot disintegrate."

JOHN STEINWAY, LONG ISLAND CITY, NY

EMPLOYEE AT STEINWAY & SONS PIANOS, LONG ISLAND CITY, NY

EMPLOYEES AT STEINWAY & SONS PIANOS, LONG ISLAND CITY, NY

"There are over 12,000 parts in one piano."

JOHN STEINWAY, LONG ISLAND CITY, NY

162

"...hand-crafted methodology..."

JOHN STEINWAY, LONG ISLAND CITY, NY

"If you don't do the best you can, then you just shouldn't be in the business."

SAM ZYGMUNTOWICZ, BROOKLYN, NY

SAM ZYGMUNTOWICZ, BROOKLYN, NY

161

CATHY SCANLAN & KARL M. DENNIS, WARREN, RI

DENNIS G. WARING, MIDDLETOWN, CT

MICHAEL BRESLER, PROVIDENCE, RI

"When you play the flute, you have to have a good intention."

NORMAN LOPEZ, TOWOAC, CO

NATIVIDAD "NATE" TIRADO, NEW CASTLE, DE

178

DMYTRO SOROCHANIUK, PENNSAUKEN, NJ

ELIZABETH VANDER VEER SHAAK, PHILADELPHIA, PA

*"I learned the spirit
of bow making... to really
understand the wood..."*

ELIZABETH VANDER VEER SHAAK, PHILADELPHIA, PA

"With drums, you'll always be working with the truth."

DWIGHT GRAVES, WARNER, NH

"After I made my first drums, it got contageous..."

RASHEED ALI, ALTA DENA, CA

KEVIN ENOCH, BELTSVILLE, MD

189

BILL ALLEGRETTI, CLAYTON, DE

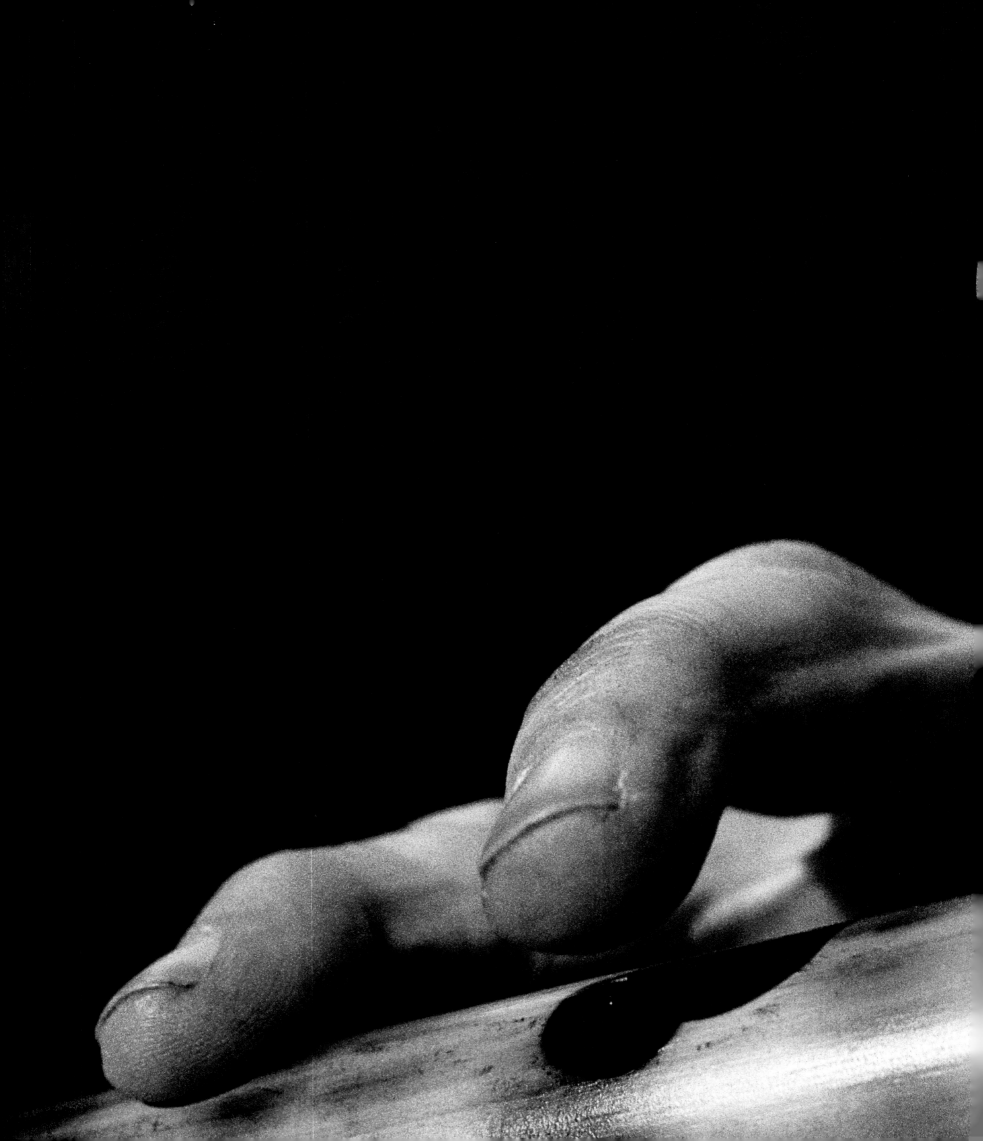

"I don't know why, but when you come close to doing exactly what you want to do, it's almost scary..."

PIERRE GOSSELIN, NEW YORK CITY, NY

THE NORTHEAST REGION

Well, yeah by accident, they have the carnival in Trinidad, so there was this guy, there were bands, and you take up anything to make a noise, a percussion, pick up somebody's trash can probably and after beating this trash can with a stick all day it got dented and he realized he was getting different sounds from the different dents and that's how it started...

TERRENCE CAMERON, PHILADELPHIA, PA

...when there's ice and snow on the ground, they can go up on a ridge and find the best old-growth, slow-growing trees on the ridge, that have the tightest grain, cut them, and this is part of a normal lumbering operation, not just for musical instruments. Fell the trees, and they built these troughs, snow troughs, and they'd slide them down the side of the mountain for 10,000 yards. There'd be guys that sat down at the bottom of the hill listening to the logs as they whistled down the troughs. The ones that made the whistling noise, they use as musical woods, and that's the kind of thing that Stradivarius would buy, the special logs that whistled when they came down the hillside...

MARTIN GUITARS, CHRISTIAN MARTIN IV, NAZARETH, PA

It all started in what was then Constantinople in Turkey with the original family member, Abidis I. He was actually an alchemist and a cymbal maker and during his metallurgical experiments he found a way of combining copper and tin in such a way that made a very sweet, special and powerful-sounding cymbal, and that's the same secret that they use today. Same alloy...

ZILDJIAN CYMBALS, NORWELL, MA

I have no idea why I tried something this late in the game—I mean this late in my years. It was a love for it, it's just a driven obsession for something that time played no part in. I come to work and somebody has to call me, "it's time to go home..."

BILL TIPPIN, MARBLEHEAD, MA

When you make a violin, you can't compromise. The biggest thing is you really can't compromise on a musical instrument like you can on an automobile. By that I mean, instead of using a lot of chrome all over the thing you get into plastics and you get into cheaper things and light weight and this and that. With these instruments, you really can't. They're made out of wood. They took the same amount of time to make this instrument as it took a luthier maybe 200 years ago to make it.

PETER KYVELOS, BELMONT, MA

There are some days I walk about here shaking my head and wonder why do I build bagpipes. And then there are days when everything comes down here and the stars are right and the sun is right, and you're holding your feet right, and what not, and everything just seems to work—that's why I build bagpipes. *And* the fact that you work for yourself.

It enables some people to live longer, happier lives. And if I'm doing just a small amount to add to that, I'm gonna keep trying. You know, I've got another ten years before I could retire, if you want to call it that, but I'll probably die slumped over my lathe...

MICHAEL S. MACHARG, SOUTH ROYALTON, VT

Don't rush things! To build a good instrument, you shouldn't rush it. Just take your time...

NATIVIDAD "NATE" TIRADO, NEW CASTLE, DE

The making of a Steinway piano is a hand-crafted operation; you do see state-of-the-art, computer machines here. This is a million dollar machine, and basically we use that kind of technology in the cutting of component parts. It enhances quality, a more precise cut and less pressure on the wood, so it's not that we don't hand-craft Steinways, it's that we use technology where it enhances quality.

These presses were an original invention of one of the sons of our founder and they were invented a little over a hundred years ago in the 1880s. It really was a giant leap forward for the piano and for Steinway. And we still do this exactly the same way as we did 100 years ago...

STEINWAY & SONS PIANOS, LONG ISLAND CITY, NY

The music is changing, that's for sure. But, still, you get down in them mountains—they still got that bluegrass music. The real stuff. I started carving little miniature guitars... It's all I ever wanted to do. I'd lay awake at night dreaming how to make guitars. And then one day I made my first real guitar...

BOB BENEDETTO, EAST STROUDSBERG, PA

But, it's nice up here, I really like it. We have a few people around town, we kind of get together on Saturday nights and play pool and play poker. A lot of guys come over and help me burnish. You have to burnish these pots; it takes a long time to burnish them you know.

The drum, you know, that's my medicine.

People two years ago bought some of my whistles and their friends came back and said they'd used their whistles. They work at sea and they used them to call the whales. And I said what kind of whistle was it. And they said, "A whale whistle." ...They're also really good for owls. Owls really like'em a lot...

When I got back from Vietnam, I kind of howled at the moon for about a year and now I'm calling owls on my whistle. I'm starting to put it together...

So, it took me a long time to figure how to build these drums right and get them to talk... Teach how to express yourself below your shoulders. That's what's so nice about drums. Art. Drums are your heart space—that's truth, you know. Like the fire-walk, you'll always be working with *truth*...

DWIGHT GRAVES, WARNER, NH

...I learned the spirit of bow making and not measuring things, but using your body, to sense the wood, using your fingertips and using the deflection in your hands to really understand the wood instead of getting caught in using your calipers to measure. And it's a whole different concept...

ELIZABETH VANDER VEER SHAAK, PHILADELPHIA, PA

Once you get into the guitar making field, there's a hook that doesn't let you go. Look at this piece of wood. I could take that piece of wood, I could thin it down, I could shape it, I could mold it—*then* I could make it play music. And then it will make other people hear and feel good, and get the feeling out of that piece of wood, that was just static before, just there... So, I get chills thinking about it because it's just really wonderful...

FRANK FINOCCHIO, EASTON, PA

...So by doing this music, by teaching people about our traditions...this is an outlet — it makes me feel proud of what I am. Makes me love more my culture. Our cultures belong to this hemisphere...

JUAN "PEPE" SANTANA, STANHOPE, NJ

So many people say to us, "Oh gee, I didn't know anybody even made those anymore. You guys actually have a business doing this? You make a living." And we say, "No, we don't make a living, but we do it anyway..."

C. B. FISK ORGAN COMPANY, GLOUCESTER, MA

The other secret to aesthetic success—is not the tool itself, but it's what you bring to it. I have seen the simplest of instruments, two sticks, simple, like one-stringed instruments, just play the most incredible soulful, meaningful, stimulating music in the world. Because the person brought some imagination to it and their soul. And that's a magic combination. So when I run out of money and I'm crying the blues, I have to remind myself that there are other ways of being paid, and the thrill of working with my hands and the gratification that comes when I build something—and that first note...

DENNIS G. WARING, MIDDLETOWN, CT

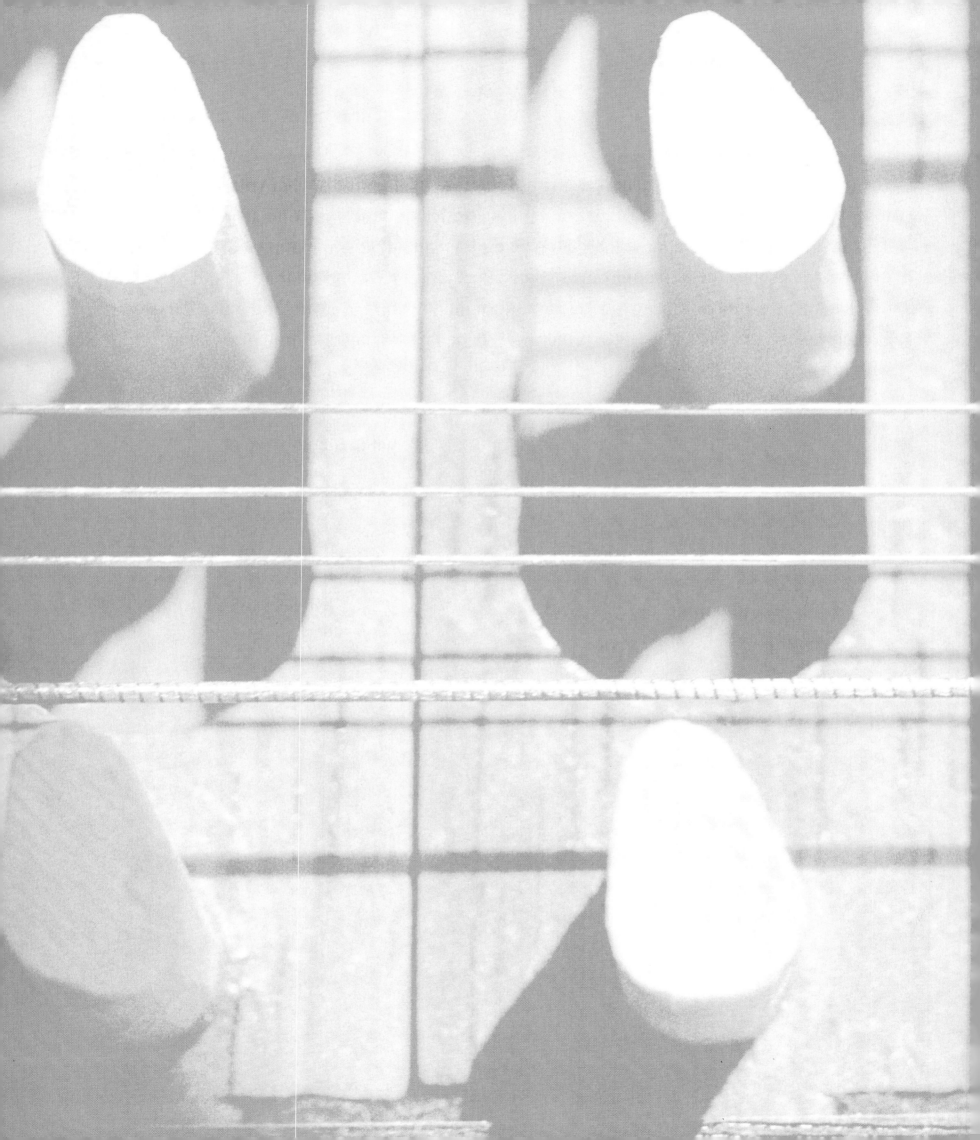

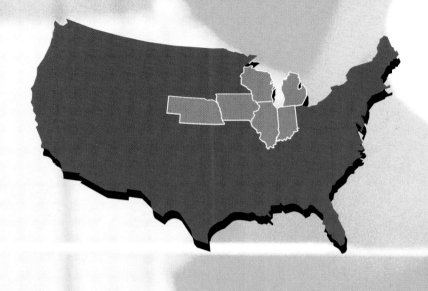

THE MIDWEST REGION

If the Delta is the source of America's soul, then the Middle West is its heart, a region which emits cultural impressions as readily as it absorbs them. This middle ground juxtaposes traditional textures north, south, east, and west. The wind gusting from the lake country carries with it uprooted seeds of creativity and sets them upon journeys to a tapestry of compass points. From industrialized urban centers to the vast sweep of its rural countryside, the Midwest—both culturally and geographically—represents the heartland of Americana.

The Industrial Revolution brought many immigrants and their centuries old musical heritage's from Europe and Scandinavia during the 1920s. Jazz, Blues, and Folk forms were created and developed. Innovative musical craftspeople set up postage stamp size studios, small factories, and even large manufacturing warehouses, eventually producing more instruments than anywhere in the world.

Midwestern craftspeople embody the spirit of national freedom and exhibit a singular combination of artistic quality and meticulous technique in their pursuit to produce the very best American musical instruments.

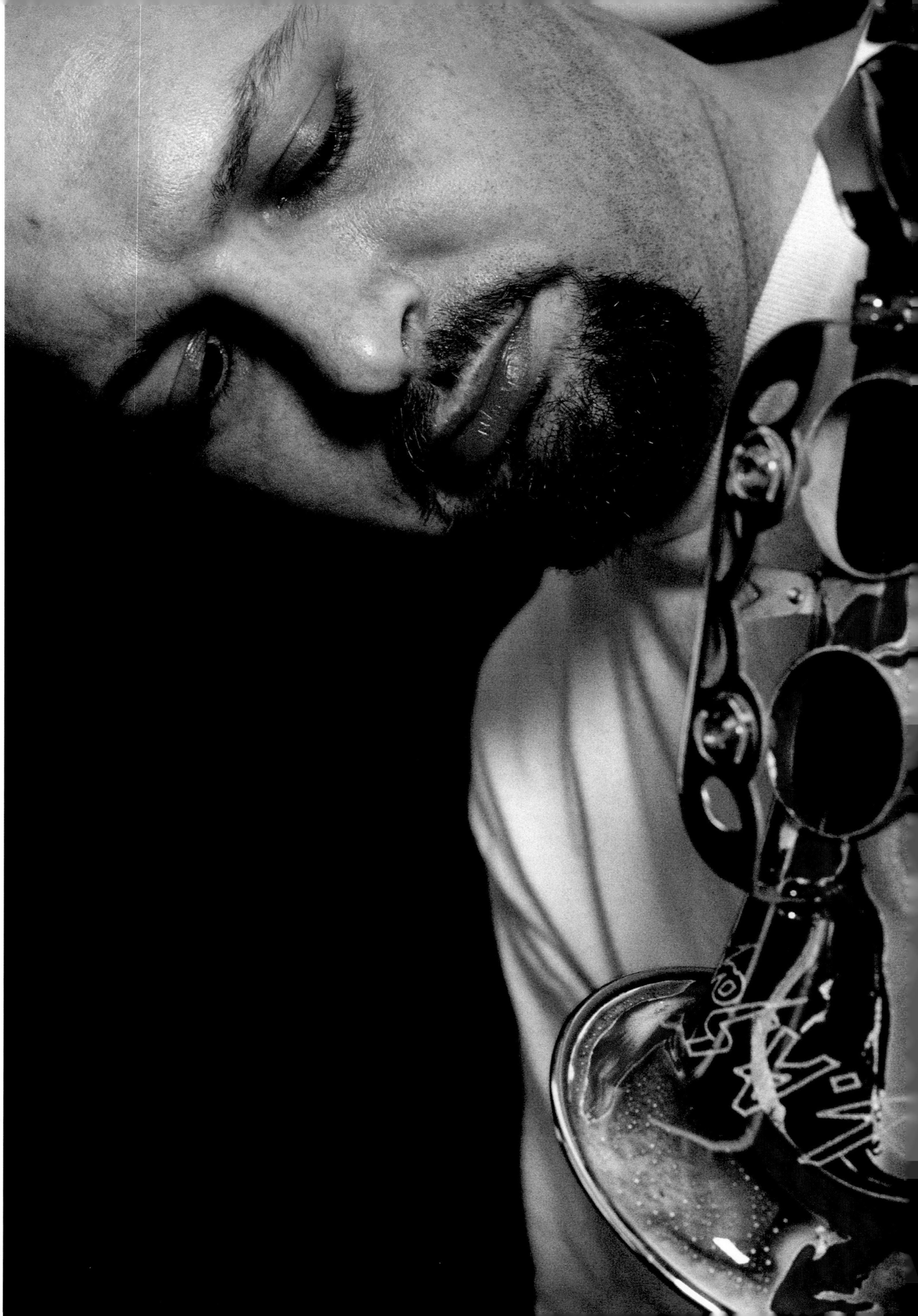

TODD AT THE
L.A. SAX COMPANY,
BARRINGTON, IL

BOB FULTON AT GETZEN CO. INC., ELKHORN, IL

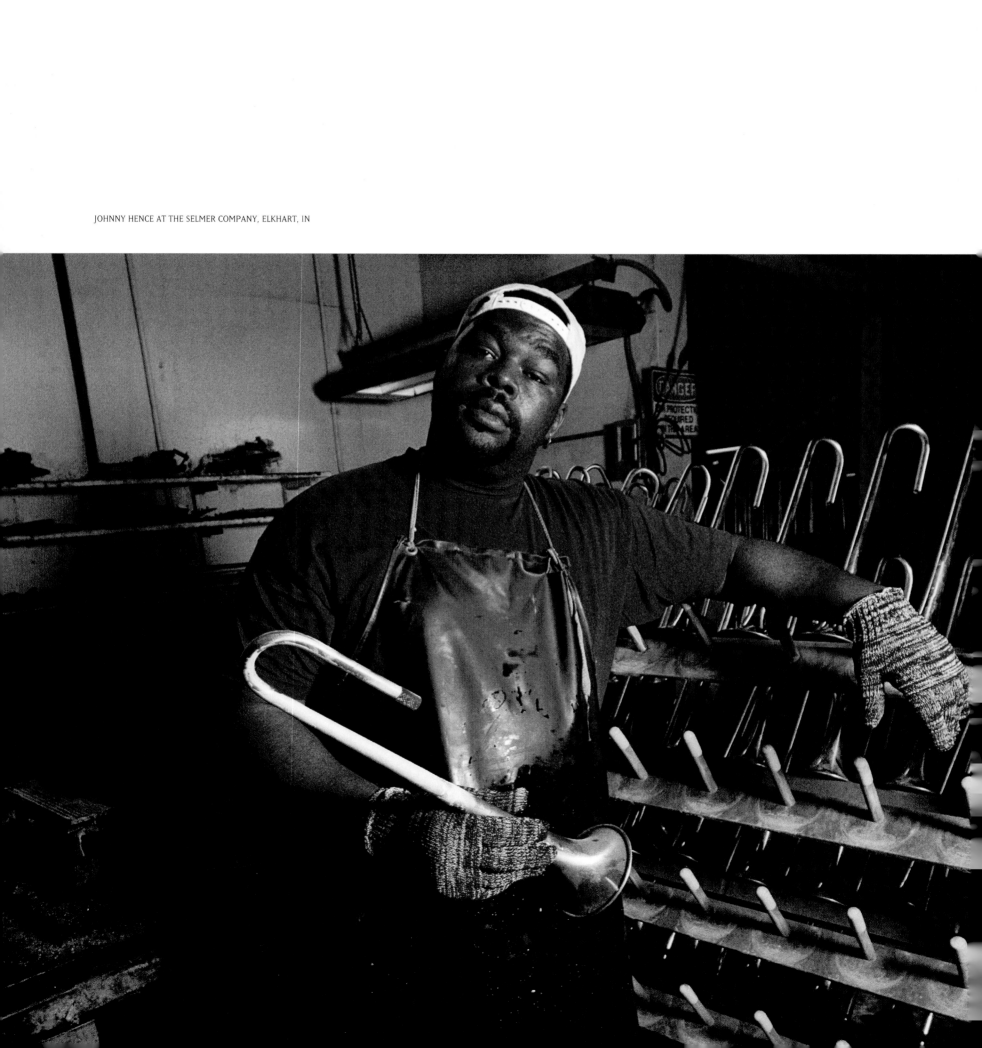

RANDY AT THE SELMER CO. INC., ELKHART, IN

"The quality in the U.S. makers is just incredible right now, and going up."

BRENDA MIRALLES, ALTA DENA, CA

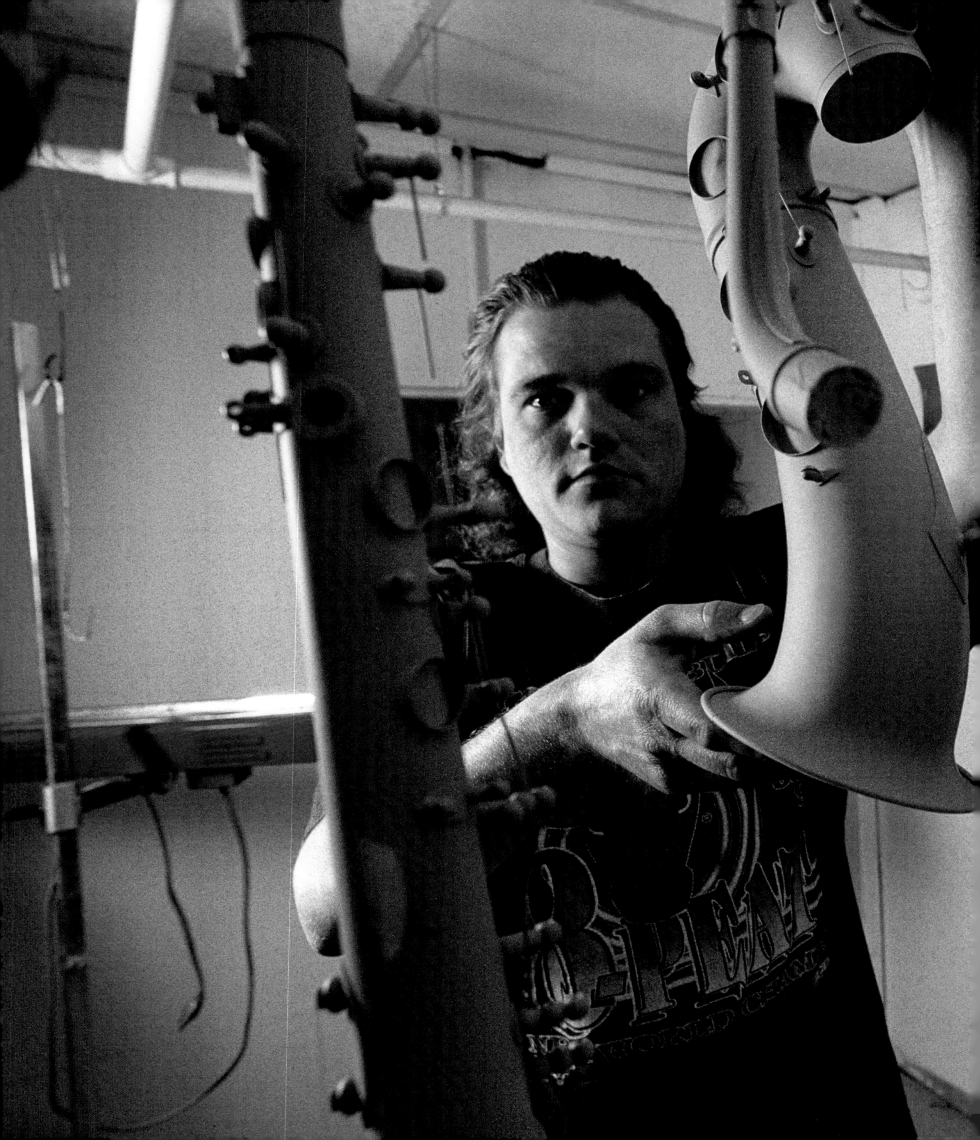

JOSÉ AT G. LeBLANC CORPORATION, KENOSHA, WI

"...It's never good enough."

JOHN ZIEDLER, PHILADELPHIA, PA

CHARLES AND FRED MELK, MELK MUSIC, MILWAUKEE, WI

LEON PASCUCCI AND
MIKE JOHNSON AT
G. LEBLANC CORPORATI
KENOSHA, WI

"... you and the guitar become one."

ROBERT L. VINCENT, TRACY DEUEL VOCATIONAL INSTITUTION, TRACY

LISA GROVER AT THE SELMER CO. INC.,
ELKHART, IN

"It's not really music as much as it is sound that is my goal."

BRETT GOLDSTONE, HIGHLAND PARK, CA

PETE LaPACA AND H ALLAN AT THE L.A. SAX CO., BARRINGTON, IL

ROBERTO SALAZAR
AT G. LeBLANC CORPORATION,
KENOSHA, WI

TERRY GRAMETZ AT THE SELMER CO., ELKHART, IN

"Don't rush things."

NATIVIDAD "NATE" TIRADO, NEW CASTLE, DE

CHARLES MABIE AT THE SELMER CO. INC., ELKHART, IN

THE MIDWEST REGION

In 1962 my grandfather sold the Getzen Company to an attorney in Milwaukee, who sold it to an accountant, who raped and pillaged the company. And on April Fool's day, 1991, my brother and I bought the company back out of the federal bankruptcy court.

The processes were actually hand written on the walls of the old factory and when they painted they painted around the processes.

The jazz trumpet design has a different type of brilliance, a different type of projection, depending on the player...

An orchestra player may need to project to the back of the hall, so he uses a different type of bell, different composition depending on what piece they're playing. So, we offer'em all the options...

GETZEN COMPANY, INC., ELKHORN, IL

First-time visitors to the factory, even knowledgeable visitors, bank directors, or whatever, who have an intimate understanding of the instruments and what they are, are always amazed — at the fact that we make the whole instrument truly from scratch, including every key, every screw, every spring...

MIKE JOHNSON, G. LEBLANC CORPORATION, KENOSHA, WI

Guitars don't have to be big to be loud. Acoustical efficiency is more important than size.

Well, there your energy is being constantly supplied. The energy is immediately being dissipated. And so, the guitar is essentially a dying instrument; you pluck the string, the sound is dying. So, the whole trick with a guitar is to have that balance between letting the energy dissipate too quickly as opposed to letting it hang too long. The quicker it dissipates, the more initial energy you have, the louder it appears to be, because all the energy goes out like a fire cracker. And if it holds the sound too long, you don't have the apparent volume of the instrument, although it may sustain the tones for longer at a time. So, it's a balance between those two.

You go back and study the makers of France in the 18th century, it's exactly the way they were conducting business, no difference—no difference at all. My social status is exactly the same. Things don't change.

Gypsies from Spain created the flamenco music. Their guitars were usually made out of cypress. That's one of the few woods that grows in Spain that's suitable for making guitars. With the Gypsies, flamenco music is primarily about death. And so the poetic justice of having a tree associated with death, which was used for making caskets, to shade the cemeteries producing the guitars out of it. So that the voice of the guitar echoed the voice of the traditional, of cypress, the sound of death...

People are still really *dead* serious about music, no matter what it is...very passionate. So are the people that make the instruments—it's a shared passion which goes hand in hand. You just can't separate it...

RICHARD BRUNÉ, EVANSTON, IL

There are more musical instruments produced in Elkhart than there are anywhere else. You have the major companies in this town; Selmer, Vincent, Bach, UMI, Emerson Flute... There's a lot of second and third generation people who are involved with the music industry here. Lots of people build specialty instruments, hand made instruments in their garages. Elkhart probably has one of the lowest unemployment rates in the nation.

This is one of the few industries that's still a hand-crafted industry. You can't learn how to do it in school — it's a hands-on experience that's passed from person to person, from father to son, from mother to daughter, and so on. I learned when I was 15 years old...

JOHN HERKENRODER, UNITED MUSICAL INSTRUMENT USA, INC., ELKHART, IN

He traced its roots back to Selmer, Paris. That was a family business — still is. It goes back to the 1800s, and there were two brothers... In the early 1900s, one of them came to the United States — he played in the New York Philharmonic. He had a small store in New York that was importing the family instruments. He hired a guy in New York City to be the store manager; he was a musician and repair guy, named George Bundy... He started Selmer USA in the 1920s and we moved to Elkhart in the 1920s and we've been here since.

In the 1920s George Bundy wanted to expand beyond just being an importer in New York City — he wanted to start making instruments in the U.S. He moved to Elkhart then, because there was this skilled labor pool here that knew how to make instruments....

THE SELMER COMPANY, INC., ELKHART, IN

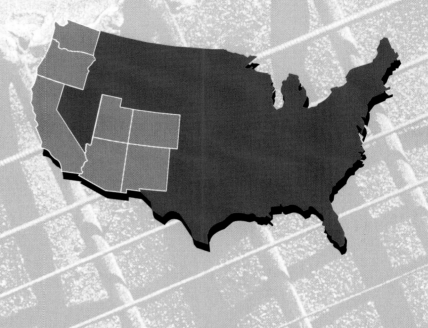

THE WESTERN REGION

The West is less about the American Dream than it is about the dreams of most Americans in their pursuit of

something vaguely better. Whether by wagon train or railroad, pioneers discovered a new land which eventually took

its influences not only from the East but from the South as well as Mexico and Central and South America. Saguaro cactus

to Monterey pine, the path snaking through the great expanse that is the American West has always been a journey into

the unknown, but closer to destiny. Every Western highway has a terminus; the route is often an adventure of discovery.

From the Native American flute and drum makers of the Southwest to the avant garde craftsmen and performers

of the West Coast to the unique California prison system instrument making program, this region is at once a reflection

of the traditional and the new. In the Pacific Northwest one can trace a direct path out of the dense forest to some of

the finest musical woodworkers in the country.

Rocks. Sun. Trees. Animal life. The Western landscape serves as an inspiration for many instrument makers, and

especially for the region's Native Americans who approach their craft from ancient and long-renewed spiritual traditions.

"Music bridges all the gaps...
It's the heartbeat,
the international language."

DWIGHT GRAVES, WARNER, NH

231

JOHN L. ZEHNDER, LOS ANGELES, CA

"And it's all surprise, so you have to experiment... it becomes an engagement with the unexpected."

RICHARD COOKE, MOAB, UT

RICHARD COOKE, MOAB, UT

DON YOUNG,
AT NATIONAL GUITARS
SAN LUIS OBISPO, CA

23

239

240

"...its just you and the guitar... nobody else around you exists..."

ROBERT L. VINCENT, TRACY DEUEL VOCATIONAL INSTITUTION, TRACY, CA

243

245

OLIVER DiCICCO, SAN FRANCISCO, CA

GEORGE ABE, LOS ANGELES, CA

"Once you make the "Why?" decision to do kinetic work, ...You're completely free to invent."

BRETT GOLDSTONE, HIGHLAND PARK, CA

"It's not me; it's the Great Spirit
who we listen to... and the presence
of this Maker, coming upon all of us."

NORMAN LOPEZ, UTE MOUNTAIN TRIBE RESERVATION, TOWOAC, CO

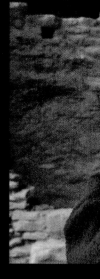

NORMAN LOPEZ, UTE MOUNTAIN TRIBE RESERVATION, TOWOAC, CO

FRANK MIRABAL, TAOS PUEBLO, NM

"I know who I am, where I've come from."

ROBERT MIRABAL, TAOS PUEBLO, NM

ROBERT MIRABAL, TAOS PUEBLO, NM

"The drum — toom-toom — that's pretty much the way your heart goes."

DWIGHT GRAVES, WARNER, NH

PIERSON MITCHELL, WARM SPRINGS RESERVATION, WARM SPRINGS, OR

260

ELA LAMBLIN, SEATTLE, WA

"...I would look... and I would dream...."

MURRAY HUGGINS, ASHLAND, OR

MARIO & BRENDA
MIRALLES,
ALTA DENA, CA

264

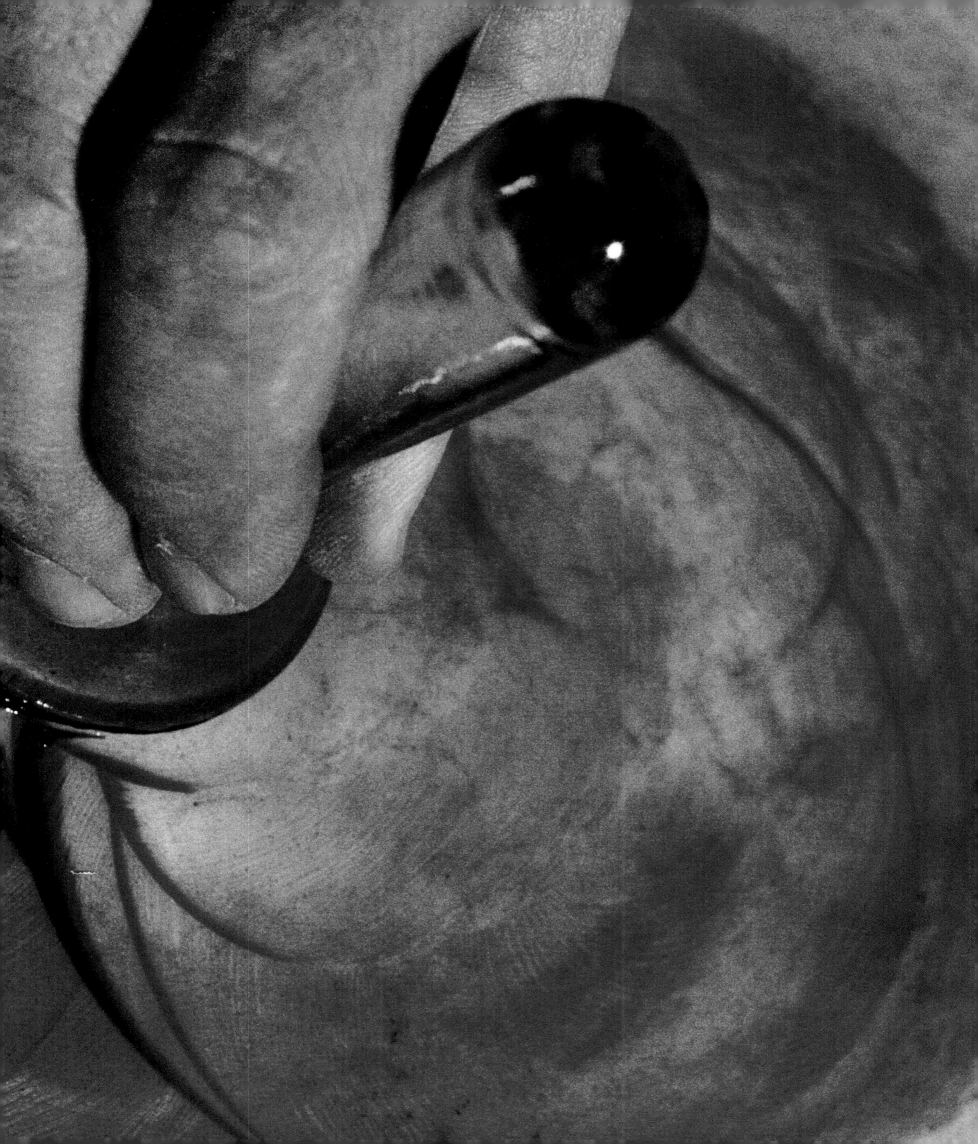

TIMOTHY NORTH,
SAN FRANCISCO, CA

"Music is not only good for children,
it's good for the human being."

CONSTANDINO "DINO" BERSIS, NEW YORK CITY, NY

"This has given me food,
given me shelter, it has given me life."

ROBERT MIRABAL, TAOS, NM

268

THE WESTERN REGION

Like a saxophone, you basically have to blow; when you stop blowing it stops making a sound. Your whole body, your whole nervous system and the liquid ocean of your blood, is all vibrating, set into sympathetic vibration by these tones...

I used to swim with the whales, and you hold your breath and go down and they start singing their song—it goes right through your body and it moves your entire body. I notice this sound had a lot of the same effects.

But, I've deliberately made instruments that have notes randomly ordered, so that the predictive tendency of the mind is thwarted, or is alleviated, so you can just go straight into play, like a child. A child doesn't know pattern. They discover pattern...

RICHARD COOKE, MOAB, UT

The best sound radiating material in the world is Styrofoam...

BART HOPKIN, NICASIO, CA

I do believe that drum making is a craft that should be shared with future generations. Very early in life, my grandfather taught me that the drum represented the heart-beat of the earth...

PIERSON MITCHELL, WARM SPRINGS, OR

The heartbeat of the world is the drum. So to make the animal live, we must make the *dead* animal come alive. That's the meaning down in the drum...

JULIUS "JUNO" LEWIS, BOYLE HEIGHTS, CA

I want to see some musical appreciation, so what better way than to make instruments? I mean what better way to learn music appreciation than to appreciate how sound is made, period.

Something that's happened for thousands of years, taking a skin and wetting it and stretching it over a vessel.

...so all this organic stuff...I think that connects kids. This is not Nintendo, this is not this controlled environment — this is really something very earthy...

RASHEED ALI, ALTA DENA, CA

Humans kind of need to work at themselves to not get stuck in their thinking about things... We tend to want to get complacent, not challenge things — but it's so exciting if you do, you know...So exciting and that's how you come up with new stuff. It's wonderful.

We're looking at all the traditional limitations and trying to figure out which of them are important, which of them are vital to what we want the end product to be and which of them we can just get rid of, or ignore, or twist a little, or whatever. So it's kind of fascinating, that aspect of it, working with the limitations of the traditional and pushing them, expanding them...

FRED CARLSON & SUZY NORRIS, SAN LUIS OBISPO, CA

I am continually challenged...

MICHAEL PERKINS, BEN LOMAND, CA

What I'm in here for is first-degree murder. I have a 25 or life sentence. When I'm gonna get out—don't know. Some time in the near future...

I get a lot of personal satisfaction out of completin' a guitar. We start with just raw boards, we re-saw everything and, I mean we start with this lumber and then create this beautiful instrument that sounds good and looks good. It's pretty rewarding. I think it helped with patience. It takes a lot of patience and discipline to really get it down.

At first I wasn't too sure. But I've gotten into buildin' these guitars so much that I want to do it when I get out. I mean, I can't imagine not buildin' guitars now. I just love doin' it. It's an option for me when I get out.

Working with this, it teaches you patience and at the same time you devote yourself, well actually, you put yourself into the guitar, you know. You and the guitar more or less become one as time goes.

It teaches you patience and it gives you...it builds up your self esteem in a lot of ways. You can look at these guitars and compare to what we have up on the wall, and the finished product—it does something for you. Because you look at it and say, "I accomplished this—I did this," knowin' that you're able to give something back even though you *took* something from society. At the same time, we're tryin' to redeem ourselves. To show'em that I'm not that same youngster back then.

There's a difference between then and now. Then, I was just a youngster runnin' around; now, I'm a mature adult and I make better decisions.

It's really a privilege to be a part of this program.

And to me the *inside* is really the most beautiful part of it. We spend a lot of time on the inside of a guitar and that's never even seen.

By makin' it, you get this inner peace from inside, because it's just you and the guitar. Nobody else around you exists. It's like you build a relationship with the wood. And you start to understand what it needs and at the same time it helps you understand what other people need to help nurture them along—and yourself. It's helped me a lot and I wouldn't mind doin' it when I get out...

ROBERT L. VINCENT, TRACY DEUEL VOCATIONAL INSTITUTION, TRACY, CA

I really do get into the fact that it's bamboo too—natural. It grows up out of the ground, bamboo is just so incredibly useful wherever it's found. Historically and otherwise, when man came into the Pacific rim, you could eat the shoots, building material, like build huts with it, you could hollow it out very easily—you could make pipes...

GEORGE ABE, LOS ANGELES, CA

The music of the instrument of a drum, it represents tone, walkin' on the earth, the beat of the earth. Like inside your heart, the heart inside of your body, that's like what tone's inside the mother earth. Any way you beat on the drum, it's the same thing as being inside the earth. Be a warrior, be a dancer...

DARRELL BENALLY, MONUMENT VALLEY, AZ

The significance in the dream about being an instrument builder and a musician is that you bring what culture you can offer to a community and try to exploit it as much as you possibly can, meaning that you share it with as many people as you know. It makes the lifestyle much more special for the people who are living in the community. And that's why too, being an artist is so important. Without artists, it'd be a real drag....

MURRAY HUGGINS, ASHLAND, OR

It's a hard way to make a living. I'm still learning how to do that, but I've kinda gotten to a point in my life where I feel like it's the best thing I do—and the most important thing I do and the thing I want to do the most. So I hope to be able to continue doing it for as long as I can....

JOEL ECKHAUS, PORTLAND, OR

So, it's like basically structure and chaos. So, the way that I look at it is, what I'm doing is purposefully balancing these two systems of structure and chaos and by using rhythm, I'm able to set up a system of composing a piece that brings people in on something that they understand in structure, and bring it in to the point where then, all of a sudden, because it's a fast rhythm, at a particular point it breaks down and turns into chaos. You're brought into it. If you're led into it through an aspect of slowly bringing you into that and then you're inside of it, you have a totally different understanding of where you're at...

SCOT JENERIK, SAN FRANCISCO, CA

My grandparents were flute makers. The Ute people didn't allow ladies to give flute music and there was a ritual that only men could make flutes and that's because we attract attention. It had its own love potion that went with it. There was not such a thing as automobiles, airplanes. You could hear a flute player quite a ways off into the distance.

It was all natural and the way it was made, it was made through the wind...

Other people cannot play your flute, but they say that when you play the flute you must have a good intention—if you feel bad you can't be playing the flute.

You make a flute when you're at an early age. At first what you do is you watch and listen, listen to the stories, then you begin to touch and understand to make the flute. Then you're told how and when to go out and get the wood you need. What kind of herbs and things that you need to gather for that—what offering you must give and how much offering you must give to take this...and to play the flute accordingly....

NORMAN LOPEZ, TOWAOC, CO

You look at music, you look at other things, language, culture, relationship, kinship, stuff like that. Then you'll will find that there is commonality between cultures all over the world...

CLYDE BENNALLY, MESA VERDE PARK, CO

Acknowledgements

The work involved in a project of this kind is vast. So many people have contributed so much to help make this book a reality—it has involved literally hundreds of people. Here is an attempt to thank some of them in writing:

First and foremost I would like to thank the great people whom we photographed. This book, of course, would not be possible without you. Thank you for your time, your energy, your wonderful work and your friendship. I hope in some small way it pays tribute to who you are and what you have dedicated your life to accomplishing.

Many thanks for all their efforts also go to:

Mary Batten Jacobson, for the great opportunity she has given to me and so many others.

Trisja Malisoff whose limitless energy, talent and perseverance have helped bring this project to its completed state.

Sam Abell, National Geographic photographer, for his inspiration and guidance.

All the staff and students at The Santa Fe Photographic Workshops.

Ruth and Mike Verbois, Shukri Farhad and the staff at Media 27 for the excellent production and help in all aspects of creating and printing this book.

David Griffing, book designer, Media 27, for his excellent designs and great sense of humor that made all the hard work almost fun.

Ernest Brooks II and all my friends at Brooks Institute of Photography for their support over the years.

My staff at Northlight of Colorado for all their great work and patience with me.

Dale Wilson for his outstanding expertise in so many areas and his important friendship to me.

Bill Ying and Andrew Reiner for their financial and legal guidance and friendship.

Lisa Cory and Joanne Barham for their fine photo assistance and great company on the road.

A&I Color in Los Angeles for the finest Kodachrome processing anywhere.

Jan Wieringa for her guidance and encouragement.

John and Vera Krausz, for all their wonderful friendship, guidance and encouragement.

Keith Addis for his guidance, friendship and advice over the years.

Phil Joanou for his encouragement, friendship and artistic knowledge.

Michael Cullen for his friendship and help on all things photographic.

Sid Jacobs, Clay Jenkins, Lee Secor and Oscar Brashear for all their wonderful music, help and inspiration.

Nancy Campbell, for her friendship and all she contributes to my life.

All the folks at the Smithsonian Institution for their enthusiasm and belief in this project, including Smithsonian Institution Exhibition Service (SITES) staff: Anna Cohn, Director; Frederica Adelman, Lawrence Hyman, Fredric Williams and Karen Whitehair. Also thanks to James Weaver at the National Museum of American History.

Könemann Publishing and the staff for publishing this book without compromising any important quality aspects.

Robert Bailey, David Debs and Nancy Ellis for their excellent editing and writing efforts.

Dr. Billy Taylor for his interest in these important people and his outstanding foreword of this book.

My mother, Miriam Jacobson, and all my friends and family who have been so encouraging and supportive.

Acknowledgements

Alabama

Alabama Center for Traditional Arts
    Aimee Schmidt

Alabama Center for Traditional Culture
    Henry Willet

Alabama State Council of the Arts
    Joey Brackner — Folklife Program
    Georgina Clarke

Joyce Coutman

California

Robert Bailey

David Begliner

Brian Bibby — Native American Specialist

Bowers Museum

California Arts Council
    Tom Chin — Sacramento
    Howard Lazar — San Fransisco
    Amy Kitchner — Fresno Arts Council
    Barbara Rham — Sacramento

California Film Commission Permit Office
    Pam Lockheart

Cindy Clark — Media 27

Nancy Covey

Cultural Affairs Department City of Los Angeles
    Joan DeBruin — Folk Arts Affairs
    Mark Greenfield — Watts Tower Director
    Terry Liu — Long Beach Folk Arts

Cultural Council of Santa Cruz County
    Lynn Magruder — Executive Director

Paul De Marinis

Beverly Gladstone

J.R. Hall III

Bess Hawes — CA NEA State Coordinator

Bart Hopkins

Humbolt Arts Council
    Debbie Goodwin — Executive Director

Sid Jacobs

Japanese American Cultural Center
    Jerry Yoshitomi — Director
    Robert Hori — Education Director

McCabes Music Store

Quentin Dart Parker

JP Peterson

Reso — Phonic National Guitars

Salano State Prison
    Armando Cid — Institutional Artist Facilitor
    Lt. Robert Wong — Public Info Officer

San Fransisco Arts Commission, State of California
    Richard Newirth — Dir. of Cultural Affairs

San Luis Obispo County Arts Council
    Barbara Roche — Director
    Lorraine — assistant

Santa Barbara Trust for Historic Preservation
    David Debs — Curator

Sound Sensation Foley Group

Southwest Indian Museum

Sue Stanberger

State of California Correctional Department
    Tip Kendal — Assistant Director of Communication
    Angela Dawson

Senshin Buddist Temple

Silver Lake Travel
    Donna Mori
    Linda Oda
    Sachi Oda

Jamie Theis

Kevin Theis

Patty Theis

Tracy Prison / Deuel Vocational Institutional (DVI)
    Steven Emrick — Institutional Arts Director
    Lt. Cindy Lincoln — Public Info Officer

UCLA Musicology Department
    Ray Giles — Museum Curator and Scientist
    Alden Ashford — Professor
    John Bishop — California Crossroads Project /
      World Arts & Culture

Ventura County Arts Council
    Susan Feller

Jill Walsh

John Walsh — Director — Getty Museum

Bill Wood

Colorado

Anazasi State Park
    Darrell Bennally

Laura Anderson

Bob Davis

Alexander Dolinin

Ute Mountain Tribe Reservation

Dale Wilson

Connecticut

Connecticut Commission of Arts
    John Ostrout

Folkcraft Instruments Store
    David & Melissa Marx

Institute for Community Research
    Lynne Williamson

Dennis Waring

Delaware

Delaware Division of Arts
    Peggy Amsterdam — Director
    Susan Sulki

Delaware Folklife Program
    Micheal Miller

Gregory Jenkins

Gonzalez Martinez — Hispanic Community Co.

District of Columbia

D.C. Commission on Arts & Humanities
    Mike Licht

National Council for Traditional Arts
    Joe Wilson — Director

National Endowment for the Arts
    Dan Sheehy

Smithsonian Institution American Folkways Program
    Tony Seger — Folk Ways Dept. & Archives

National Museum of American History, Smithsonian
Institution — James Weaver

Smithsonian Institution Traveling Exhibition Service

The Library of Congress
    Judith A. Gray — Reference Specialist

Thelonious Monk Institute of Jazz
    Shelby Fischer

Florida

Bureau of Historic Preservation
    Tina Bucuvalas — Dept. of Historical Resources

Museum of Florida
    Brent Tozzer

Southern Arts Foundation
    Peggy Folger

Georgia

Georgia Council for the Arts
    Maggie Holtzberg — Folklife Program

Georgia Music Hall of Fame
    Joseph Johnson — Curator

University of Georgia
    Art Rosenbaum

Illinois

Illinois Arts Council
    Loretta Rhoades — Director of Folk & Ethnic Arts

Old Town School of Folk Music
    Jim Hirsch — Executive Director

The L.A. Sax Co.
    H Allan

Indiana

Indiana Arts Commission
    Dorothy Ilgen
    Cliff Lambert

United Music Instrument Company
    Chris Neidhamer
    John Herkenroder
    Rich Breske

The Selmer Co., Inc.
    Vince McBride — EVP
    David Mester — VP

Iowa

Iowa Arts Council
    Riki Saltzman

Iowa City Library
    Rosie Springer

State Historical Society of Iowa
    Steve Ohrn — Historic Sites Program

Kentucky

Tom Adler — Folklorist

Amsterdam House Violin Shop

Apple Shop
    Pam Martin
    Jim Branson

Donna Boyd

Jim Gastin

Hometown Music
    Doc Frasier

International Bluegrass Festival
    Dan Hays — Executive Director

Kentucky Arts Council

Kentucky Center for the Arts

Kentucky Council for the Arts
    Debbie Shannon — Education Dept.

Kentucky Folklife Program
    Robert Gates

Ron Penn — Appalachian Music Professor

University of Kentucky
    Dr. Ashworth — Dean of Music

University of Kentucky — Archive
    & Musical History Dept.
    Richard Griscom — Industrial Arts Dept.
    Frank Pittman

Louisiana

Louisiana Folklife Center
    Don Hatley

Louisiana Folklife Program — Division of the Arts
    Maida Owens — Office of Program Development

University of Louisiana Library

Deborah-Helen Viator

Maine

Maine Arts Commission
    Kathleen Mundell — National Arts Associate

Maine Arts Festival
    Burl Hash

Portland Symphony Office

Nate Solobodkin

Maryland

National Council for the Traditional Arts
    Andy Wallace

National Endowment for the Arts, Washington D.C.
    Barry Bergey
    Dan Sheehy

Smithsonian Folk Ways Department
    Tony Seger — Department Director

State Arts Council of Maryland
    Charlie Camp — Folklorist

Massachusetts

Zildjian Cymbals
    Colin Schofield

C.B. Fiske Organs Inc.
    Greg Bover

Powell Flutes
    Geneieve Cross
    Geraldo Discepolo
    Steven A. Wasser

Michigan

Michigan Council for the Arts and Cultural Affairs
    Betty Boone — Executive Director

Michigan State University
    Kirt Dewhurst
    Marsha McDowell

Michigan Traditional Arts Program
    LuAnne Kozuma

Minnesota

Minnesota State Arts Board
    Philip Nusbaum

Folk Arts Program

Mississippi

Academy of Ancient Music
    Rich McGuinness
    Betty Jackson

Agricultural Museum
    Sandra Melsheimer

Ancient Ways
    Anderas Scott

Archives and History of Mississippi State

Bluegrass Society
    Bill Rodgers

Dr. Chuck Borum — Natchez Indian Doctor

Craftsmans Guild of Mississippi

Delta Blues Museum, Clarksdale, MS
    John Rusky — Curator

Jackson County Arts Council
    Renee and Martha

Mississippi Arts Commission
    Betsy Bradley — Executive Director
    Deborah Boykin — Folk Arts Director

Mississippi Indian Reservation, Tribal Office
    Ted Ferguson — Tribal Councilman
    Choctaw Indians
    Martha Ferguson

Mississippi State Capital

Old Courthouse Museum
    Vicksburg, Mississippi

Natchez Crafts Fair
    Pat Stroud
    Fay Arnold

Rooster Blue Records
    Jim O'Neal

School of Southern Culture,
    Mississippi University, Oxford, MS
    Dr. Bill Farris
    Scott McCraw
    Tom Rankin
    Warren Steel
    Ed Komara — Head of Blues Archives

Southern Cultural Heritage Museum
    Dinah Lazor

Vicksburg, Mississippi Historical Society
    Gordon Cotton

Missouri

Missouri Arts Council
    Flora Maria Garcia
    James Olson

Missouri Historical Society

University of Missouri
    Dana Everts — Boehm

Nebraska

Doris Marxhausen

New Hampshire

Randy Armstrong

Fiddlers Choice

New Hampshire State Council of the Arts
    Audrey Slyvester

University of New Hampshire
    Jill Linzee in Bert Finetuck's office

Vintage Fret Shop
    David Colburn

New Jersey

Casa Latin Music

International Institute of New Jersey
    Bill Westerman — Folklorist

Gregory Jenkin

Jomi Matos

New Jersey Historical Commission
    David Cohen — Folk Arts Coordinator

New Jersey State Arts Council
    Rita Moonsammy — Folk Art Coordinator

Roberto Rivera

Rutgers University — American Studies Program
    Angus Gillispie

New Mexico

Fran and Peggy Gorman

Ken Keppeler & Jeanie McCleary

Taos Pueblo Reservation

Taos Pueblo Police Department
    Janet Jackson

New York

Casitas
    Benny Ayala

City Lore
    Steve Sightman
    Roberta Singer

Ethnic Folk Arts Center
    Ethel Rahm

Folkcraft Instruments

Bob Godfried

Nancy Groce — Music Ethnologist

David Massengale

David McKean

Metropolitan Museum
  Kenneth Moore

New York State Council of the Arts Folklife Program
  Robert Baron

Pan Rebels

Bruce Pollin

Queens Council for the Arts
  Ilana Harlow

Serge Rogosin

Miquel Sierra

Steinway & Sons Pianos
  John Steinway
  Leo Spellman

Urac Indian Museum
  Tom Elliot

North Carolina

Handmade in America
  Becky Anderson

John C. Campbell Folk School
  Jan Davidson
  David Brose

North Carolina Arts Council — Folklife
  Department of Culture
  Mary Regan
  Wayne Martin

McIntrye Shop

Southern Highland Craft Guild
  Laurie Huttunen

WCQS Radio
  Jim McGill

Ohio

Liz Haroff — Folklorist

Ohio Arts Program
  Barbara Bayless — Traditional &
    Ethnic Apprentice Program
  Judy Chalker — Traditional & Ethnic Arts
  Wayne Lawson — Executive Director

Ohio Arts Program Council
  John Seto — Coordinator

Oregon

Arts Council of Oregon
  Michael Faison — Assistant Director

Buy & Sell Music Store

Cripple Creek Music

Joseph Deiss

Musician's Friend

Oregon Historical Society /
    Oregon Folklife Program
  Layla Childs
  Nancy Nusz — Folklife Program Coordinator

University of Oregon, Eugene
  Mark Levy — Music Department

Pennsylvania

Commonwealth of Pennsylvania Council of Arts
  Philip Horn — Executive Director

Amy Gabriel — Musical Coordinator

Governer's Heritage Affairs Commission
  Folklife Program

Martin Guitars
  Dick Boak

Mobile Music
  Dave LaRue

Vintage Shop
  Fred Oster
  Katherine Jacobs

Rhode Island

Betty Bernal

Rhode Island State Council of Arts
  Winifred Lambrecht

Ella Sekatou — Tribal Elder

South Carolina

South Carolina Arts Commission
  Lesley Williams — Folk Arts Program
  Cydney Barry — Administrative Specialist

Tennessee

Chattanooga Allied Arts
  Molly Sasse
  Doug Day

Country Music Foundation & Hall of Fame
  Ronnie Pugh — Head Reference Desk

Corner Music

Gruhn Guitars
  George Gruhn

Diane Patrick

Tennessee Arts Commission
  Robert Cogswell — Folk Arts Program

Tennessee Musician Union

Vanderbilt University
  Rob Thompson - Professor
  David Schnaufer

Vanderbilt University Music Library

Texas

Christopher Wrenn

Utah

Arts Council of Utah

Vermont

Fletcher Farms School for Arts & Crafts

Frog Hollow Folk Gallery
  Ann Myachulak

Dan MacArthur

Margaret MacArthur

Vermont Council on the Arts
  Nicolette Clarke — Executive Director

Vermont Craft Council
  Martha Fitch

Vermont Folklife Center

Jane Beck
Gregory Sharrow
Joyce

Vermont Handcrafts

Virginia

Appleseed Productions

Blue Ridge Institute of Ferrum College
  Roddy Moore

Goshen School of Music

Washington

Arts Council of Washington

Ethnic Hertiage Council

Institute of the North American West
  Richard Hart

Music Center of the Northwest

Washington Arts Council

Washington State Art Commission
  Bitsy Bidwell — Community Arts
    Development Manager

Willie Smyth

Washington State Folklife Council
  Margaret MacDonald

West Virginia

Augusta Hertitage Center
  Jerry Mills — State Apprentice Program

Town of Galax — Fiddler & Banjo Competition

Wisconsin

Cedarburg Cultural Center
  Bob Teske
  Jill Bault

G. LeBlanc Corporation
  Mike Johnson

Getzen Co. Inc.
  Ed Getzen

Barbara Lau — Folklorist

Melk Music
  Ruth Anne Melk

Wisconsin Arts Board
  Richard March
  George Tzougros

Wisconsin Folklife Office

"There's not much to life...unless you can pick up something important and give it back, and share."

TOM MORGAN, DAYTON, TN